INTELLECTUAL INTEGRITY

(Christian Glasses)

Developing a Christian Worldview

Richard B. Ramsay

Do not be conformed to this world, but be transformed by the
renewal of your mind, that by testing you may discern what is
the will of God, what is good and acceptable and perfect.
(Romans 12:2)

Intellectual Integrity (Christian Glasses)
Developing a Christian Worldview

Richard B. Ramsay

Evangelicals often suffer from a divided mind, separating "spiritual" things from "secular" things. This book is meant to help develop a Christian worldview, an integrated view of life, based on biblical principles. It will help you put on Christian "glasses," as John Calvin said, to look at subjects such as the concept of truth, our relation to culture, non-Christian worldviews, politics, economics, science, math, and art.

CONTENTS

Dedication

I would like to dedicate this book to our grandchildren. Although they are still young, they have brought us immense joy, and we love them dearly! They will grow up in a world that will change greatly after I write these lines. May the Lord grant them faith, love, wisdom, and joy!

The Author

Dr. Ramsay was a missionary in Chile for 21 years, teaching in a seminary and planting churches. There he met his wife, Angelica. They now live in Florida, and they have two adult children. For the past 25 years, they have worked internationally in distance education, traveling to teach classes and producing resources for theological education and leadership training. Richard has taught for *Universidad FLET* and *Thirdmill Seminary* and has developed many online courses.

He holds a D.Min. degree and an M.Div. from *Westminster Theological Seminary*, as well as a Th.M. from *Covenant Theological Seminary*.

Other books by the author include *The Certainty of the Faith, Am I Good Enough?, Basic Greek and Exegesis with Logos and e-Sword, Transformed Into the Image of Jesus, Catholics and Protestants, Strengthen Your Faith, Synopsis of the Bible, Putting the Pieces Together,* and *Orientation for Leaders.*

PREFACE

Although I grew up in a Christian family, I began to doubt my faith during my first course in philosophy at the university. In the midst of my spiritual pilgrimage, the Lord showed me His presence one night in the multitude of bright stars. I gave my heart to the Lord and returned to my dorm room as a renewed person. Nevertheless, I was unaware at the moment that I still needed to give my mind to the Lord also. I was attending classes in which they were teaching me subtly that I myself was the judge of the truth, that the truth was subjective and relative. I continued living a duality between my "spiritual" life and my intellectual life.

I woke up to this reality when I took a course on ethics several years later. First I thought my professor was a profound thinker, because of the way he asked good questions. He always said, "Why do you think that?" He made me aware that I needed to learn how to defend my point of view. But one day we went to listen to a well-known philosopher who was giving a conference on ethics. I was surprised by the fact that he made no effort to defend his views. He simply spewed out his opinions about one topic after another. I returned to class disillusioned, and certain that our professor would criticize him severely for that. When he asked our opinion of the conference, I held up my hand, convinced that everyone would agree with me, and said, "It was interesting, but he didn't defend his views." What do you think his response was? He replied, "Why do you think he should defend his opinions?" I couldn't believe it! I began to wonder whether the professor was really trying to make us think, or whether he himself had no clear answers. He seemed to be teaching us indirectly that we could simply decide for ourselves what was right or true.

As the semester continued, I realized that we were studying different philosophical views of ethics, but just like the speaker we heard, they didn't seem to give a convincing defense of their positions. Someone in class told a joke that might have seemed rather boring to me before taking this class, but at this time of the semester it made us all laugh, because it illustrated what we were observing. The joke is that two men were riding through the desert on their horses, when all of a sudden one of them hurls himself onto a cactus. The other man is astonished and asks him, "Why did you do that?!" Bleeding and looking confused, the poor man answers, "I don't know. It seemed like a good thing to do at the time!"

I began to question the fundamental presuppositions of my university education. I began to read the books of Francis Schaeffer, which showed me that the Bible speaks truth into every area of life and thought. I longed to develop a biblical view of everything. At the end of the semester, in my final paper, I argued that we should base our ethics on the authority of our Creator, who has given us ethical norms in the Scriptures.

Later, in seminary, Cornelius Van Til helped me to see the relativism and the pretended subjectivity of the truth in non-Christian thought. The Lord used these two authors to lead me to give not only my heart, but also my mind to Jesus Christ. It was really like a "second conversion."

Please don't misunderstand me. The Bible teaches that there is only one conversion, theologically speaking. However, some of us live our lives in such a divided way, between our Christian faith and our non-Christian way of thinking, that we need a radical change, so radical that we could call it an intellectual conversion.

After my struggles, I promised the Lord I would help others who were doubting. In fact, that is what motivated me to enter the ministry. I would like to offer this book as partial fulfillment of that promise that I made.

All Scripture quotations are taken from the *English Standard Version*, unless otherwise indicated.

Additional Notes for the 2023 Edition

This English version of the 2023 edition makes some updates and takes into account some changes that have occurred since the writing of the first edition of this book published in Spanish in 2005 (Editorial CLIE). Some people consider that "postmodern" may not be the best term to describe the world we live in, but don't have another better way to describe it. Donald A. Carson considers that postmodernism is no longer being openly advocated in many American college campuses as it was previously. However, he adds that "it has not been displaced by another identifiable movement" and that its influence is still felt, for example in considering all religions the same and in the "reluctance to think hard about good and evil...."[1]

There is also some debate about whether we should even talk about a "Christian worldview." Donald Carson mentions that "in recent years, a rising number of authors have pooh-poohed the notion of 'worldview' in general and of 'the Christian worldview' in particular. Some are suspicious of worldview reasoning on the grounds that no finite human

---

[1] Donald A. Carson, *Christ and Culture Revisited* (Grand Rapids: Eerdmans, 2012), Preface to the paperback version published in 2012. (The original hardback version was published in 2008.)

being can ever capture a true view of the world." His answer is that it doesn't mean claiming to have a perfect view. He says, "A 'worldview,' after all, is nothing other than a view of the 'world' — that is, of all reality."[2]

There are some fundamental doctrines that all Christians should hold, such as the existence of God, the Trinity, the creation, the Fall, the incarnation of Jesus, redemption in Jesus through His death on the cross and His resurrection, the Scriptures as our infallible source of truth, and Jesus' future return to establish the final form of His kingdom. In this book we will be going beyond those basic beliefs to look at other aspects of life, focusing on politics, economics, science, and the arts. From the outset, I want to make it clear that I don't pretend to have *the* Christian worldview in those extended areas. I am not an expert in any of those areas. I simply want to give examples of how to approach these subjects from a biblical viewpoint. I offer some thoughts from other writers who are experts in those areas, especially from the reformed tradition, and share some of my own reflections.

Others have expressed concern that studying a Christian worldview focuses too much on the intellect. I agree that this can be a problem, just like it often is when we study the Bible and theology. Christian education should include "head, hands and heart." We are to love the Lord with our heart, soul, mind and strength (Mark 12:30). However, I personally think that it is really important in our day to help evangelicals develop and defend a Christian worldview. This book is an effort to help us learn to love God with our minds, but I hope

---

[2] Donald A. Carson, *Christ and Culture Revisited* (Grand Rapids: Eerdmans, 2008), p. 95. Kindle Edition.

it also leads to love Him and worship Him more with the heart and to serve Him more faithfully with the hands.

Finally, some of the topics considered in this book have become a "minefield" for misunderstanding. I would ask the reader to please not try to put me in some category, some political affiliation, or some school of thought, assuming that I hold views that I may not hold. Just because I quote an author on a certain subject, and may agree on some things, does not mean I agree with everything the author says or make me a disciple of that author. My purpose is not to promote any theologian or movement, but simply help Christians become more consistent in their way of thinking, seeking truth in the Scriptures regarding all areas of thought.

CHAPTER 1
INTELLECTUAL SCHIZOPHRENIA [3]

"There is no Christian mind."
Harry Blamires [4]

Evangelicals often suffer from what I call "intellectual schizophrenia." I mean this in the sense of a *divided mind.* When we deal with a subject that we consider theological or "spiritual," we seek answers based on the teachings of the Scriptures, but when we deal with other topics such as politics, economics, science or art, for example, our opinions frequently have little to do with our Christian faith. The result is that we develop a fragmented way of thinking.

I remember listening to discussions a few years ago regarding whether the United States should be involved in a war in Iraq. Some were in favor, and others were against it. I don't mean to discuss the issue here; I just want to point out what I observed regarding the way Christians dialogued about it. I heard mostly comments about what might happen if we became involved, or what might happen if we did not become involved. People were predicting what might happen, and making a judgment based exclusively on that speculation. I didn't hear much talk about when a war is morally justified. There is a lot of literature on the subject, and there are biblical passages that orient our thinking about war, but these things didn't come up in the conversations. I was just as guilty as anybody else.

---

[3] When I was in Chile (1978-1999), one of the classes I taught in seminary for several years was called "Christian Philosophy." Some parts of this book are based on the teaching from those classes.
[4] Harry Blamires, *The Christian Mind* (Ann Arbor, Michigan: Servant Books, 1963), p. 3.

But it made me wonder, ¿why do we form our opinions on so many important subjects without reference to the Bible or our Christian convictions? Aren't we supposed to use the Scriptures to become prepared for all good works (2 Timothy 3:16-17)? I had the impression that many of us were just repeating what we had read in the paper or heard on television. Opinions were often based on "consequentialism" rather than biblical principles. That is, we speculate about what might happen, and then make our decision based on what we think would bring the best result. Furthermore, the concept of "the end justifies the means" is often used to defend our decisions.

I remember my shock when I first played basketball with my fellow students at seminary. I couldn't believe the change in personality in some of these future pastors when they walked onto the basketball court! Suddenly they were pushing and shoving and shouting at each other. They called the ball out of bounds when it wasn't really, and they became angry when they lost. I fell into the same pattern. We regressed to childish manners.

I see something similar in intellectual matters. Just as we often lack integrity in our actions, we also lack integrity in the way we think. We suddenly change identities when we walk on to the field of economy, art, music, or science.

The Cause of Our Lack of Intellectual Integrity

In part, this inconsistency is due to the secularization of public education. We are supposed to leave God outside the science classroom. They often teach the theory of evolution as if it were proven fact, and they leave no room for considering the concept of creation or intelligent design, because this would be mixing religion with science. Sometimes they teach us the conclusions of secular psychologists regarding the nature of man, without considering the Christian point of view.

In my first year of university studies, on the first day of classes, my philosophy professor asked how many of us believed in God. Out of several hundred students, only half of us raised our hands. Then he openly declared his intention: "I hope that by the end of the semester you will realize that there is no good reason to believe in God!" Thankfully, God used this challenge in my life to make me draw closer to Himself. However, it doesn't seem right that an atheist is allowed to try to convince the students of his views, while Christians are often forbidden to speak of our beliefs in similar public contexts.

We can also find in medieval theologians such as Thomas Aquinas (1225-74) historical roots of making a separation between faith and reason, leaving them as independent tools to discover truth. According to his view, we can use our reason to study nature to discover some truths, but we need faith and the Scriptures in order to understand other things. For example, in *Summa Theologiae*, he gives reasoned arguments for the existence of God,[5] but recognizes that "it is impossible to attain to the knowledge of the Trinity by natural reason."[6] John Frame explains that Aquinas distinguishes between "philosophy" and "sacred doctrine," and that for Aquinas, "philosophy is governed by human reason, sacred doctrine by faith." This might sound legitimate at first, but it leads to a separation which has been damaging in ways that he could not have foreseen.[7]

---

[5] Question 2, Article 1. See <www.newadvent.org/summa>
[6] Question 32, Article 1.
[7] John Frame, *A History of Western Philosophy and Theology* [Una historia de la filosofía y teología occidental] (Phillipsburg, NJ: P&R Publishing, 2015), p. 144-46.

This tendency is actually still strong today in Roman Catholic theology. In the encyclical that was published in 1998, "Fides et Ratio", pope John Paul II manifests his concern for the way in which reason has dominated over faith in some historical periods, producing agnosticism and relativism. Nevertheless, he still defends the "mutual autonomy" of both faith and reason. He says,

> Faith and reason are like two wings on which the human spirit rises to the contemplation of truth.[8]

> There is thus no reason for competition of any kind between reason and faith: each contains the other, and each has its own scope for action.[9]

> This is why I make this strong and insistent appeal—not, I trust, untimely—that faith and philosophy recover the profound unity which allows them to stand in harmony with their nature without compromising their *mutual autonomy*. The parrhesia of faith must be matched by the boldness of reason.[10]

Immanuel Kant, the famous philosopher (1724-1804), also highlighted a similar separation. He distinguished between the physical world and the metaphysical world, the "phenomenal" realm and the "noumenal" realm. "Pure" reason functions in the physical world that we experience with our senses, but "practical" reason functions in the metaphysical world. The physical world is determined, but there is freedom in the metaphysical world. Religion,

---

[8] Encyclica "Fides et Ratio", 1998, first paragraph.
[9] "Fides et Ratio", section 17.
[10] "Fides et Ratio", section 48.

Intellectual Integrity

morality and ethics are in the realm of the "noumena," a realm full of mystery.

Religion
Morality
Freedom

NOUMENA
PRACTICAL REASON   PHYSICAL WORLD

PHENOMENA   METAPHYSICAL WORLD
PURE REASON

Science
Experience
All determined

This can lead to an unhealthy dichotomy. Science becomes reasonable and objective, while religious issues are unknowable. Some may avoid the use of faith in the interpretation of nature, and others may avoid the use of reason in the interpretation of "religious" matters.

Finally, within the church during the 20th century, the fundamentalist movement reacted to modernist theology and its emphasis on social issues, preferring to focus on evangelism. While the stand for biblical inerrancy and conservative orthodox theology was necessary, the movement tended to give little attention to some important social and cultural issues. This inevitably meant leaving those areas to others and creating a fragmented worldview among themselves. Often conservative evangelicals have been criticized for "caring only for the soul but not the body," and for providing a comfortable "refuge from the world."

Nevertheless, we can't just blame others. We ourselves have often abandoned the battle for the truth. Naively we have put on the eyeglasses of the unbelievers to investigate the creation of God.

Harry Blamires argues that there is no longer a "Christian mind," that Christian thought has been secularized. By "Christian mind" he is not referring to individuals that think in a Christian manner, but rather a "collectively accepted set of notions and attitudes,"[11] a current of Christian thought to guide us, a school of thought with which we can dialogue. His experience is that we have to look for non-Christian friends to talk more profoundly about current events or serious literature.[12] I would like to say that he is wrong, but I think that his observation is frequently true.

Some of the most famous figures of western history have been Christians: philosopher-theologians such as Augustine and Thomas Aquinas, writers such as Dante, Dostoyevsky, and Tolstoy, artists like Rembrandt, and musicians like Bach. Nevertheless, in our age, few Christians would be named among the most famous.

Thankfully, there are exceptions. One of my favorite authors is C. S. Lewis. His children's stories have been translated and read in many countries of the world. His theological and philosophical books are of the highest level of scholarship. Lewis was a brilliant example of a Christian who expressed his worldview clearly. He proposed that our influence is even stronger when we deal with issues that are not exactly "spiritual," but with any kind of issue, giving it a Christian focus.

---

[11] Blamires, p. vii.
[12] Blamires, p. 4.

Intellectual Integrity

I believe that any Christian that is qualified to write a popular book about any science can achieve much more than any directly apologetic work. The difficulty that we face is this: We can (frequently) make people listen to the Christian point of view during a half hour or more; but as soon as they leave the room where we were giving the lecture, or lay aside our article, they are immediately submerged again in a world in which the opposite position is taken for granted.

...What we want are not more books about Christianity, but more books written by Christians about other subjects – with the Christianity latent.[13]

There are other authors who, while they are not as well-known as C. S. Lewis, they have been making important contributions to developing a Christian worldview. Francis Schaeffer was an inspiring example to many of us in his way of analyzing western thought and culture from a Christian perspective. (*The God Who is There, He is There and He is Not Silent, Art and the Bible, Genesis in Space and Time*). H. R. Rookmaaker wrote about art (*Modern Art and the Death of a Culture*). A current Spanish writer, Antonio Cruz, has made important contributions in the areas of science, sociology, and philosophy (*Postmodernidad, Sociología, Bioética cristiana, ¿Darwin mató a Dios?*). Alvin Plantiga, professor at *Notre Dame*, is a well-known Christian philosopher (*God and Other Minds, The Nature of Necessity, Warranted Christian Belief*). I could mention more, but my purpose is not to make

---

[13] *God in the Dock* (Grand Rapids: Eerdmans, 1970), p. 93. Quoted by John Fischerman in *Fearless Faith* (Eugene, Oregon: Harvest House, 2002), pp. 146, 147.

a complete list of authors.[14] However, I think we should thank them for contributing to a "Christian mind."

Finally, it would be unfair not to recognize that there are efforts made through social media, websites and magazines, as well as countless Christian colleges, institutes and seminaries in which people are encouraged to develop a Christian worldview. Thoughtful analysis of culture and current events is often heard in our pulpits as well. In general, I believe that the situation has improved in recent years. But there is still much to do.

The Biblical Challenge

The Scriptures urge us to think as Christians, to "renew our minds" and to "take every thought captive." Notice that this should also change the way we live.

Romans 12:2
Do not be conformed to this world, but be transformed by the renewal of your mind, that by testing you may discern what is the will of God, what is good and acceptable and perfect.

2 Corinthians 10:5
We destroy arguments and every lofty opinion raised against the knowledge of God, and take every thought captive to obey Christ.

---

[14] To mention others, much has been written in the area of psychology (Larry Crabb, Norman Wright, Jay Adams). Charles Colson has analyzed current events and schools of thought from a Christian perspective (*How Now Shall We Live?*). William Romanowski (*Eyes Wide Open; Looking for God in Popular Culture*), Douglas Groothuis (*Truth Decay*), and Os Guinness (*¿Dust of Death, Time For Truth, The Case for Civility*) are examples of Christian reflection about contemporary culture. Makoto Fujimura (*Art and Faith*) and Terry Glaspey (*Discovering God through the Arts*) are examples of authors writings about art. See the bibliography for other resources.

The first piece of armor that we are to put on is the "truth" (Ephesians 6:14).

When God created man, He gave him the task of "ruling" over the animals and "subduing" the earth.

Genesis 1:26-28

Then God said, "Let us make man in our image, after our likeness. And let them have dominion over the fish of the sea and over the birds of the heavens and over the livestock and over all the earth and over every creeping thing that creeps on the earth." So God created man in his own image, in the Image of God he created him; male and female he created them. And God blessed them. And God said to them, "Be fruitful and multiply and fill the earth and subdue it and have dominion over the fish of the sea and over the birds of the heavens and over every living thing that moves on the earth."

Let's imagine that mankind had not sinned. What would have happened? I think people would have developed a perfect society. Since they would have fulfilled the mandate to "be fruitful and multiply and fill the earth," we can assume that there would be billions of people. This would make certain forms of organization necessary. For example, man would have established guidelines for the exchange of products. People would have learned to cooperate in the care of their animals and in cultivating crops, possibly in the education of their children. They probably would have organized social structures to supervise the activities of the growing population. That is, they would have done many of the same things that they have done now, after the Fall, but without the damaging effects of sin. This I would call the "kingdom of God." The command to be administrators of the creation has been called the "cultural mandate," because it suggests an ongoing process of dominion over every aspect of human life.

The problem is that mankind in fact did sin and put an end to the perfect development of the kingdom of God. Now the kingdom of God must be established only after there has been an internal spiritual renewal in people. Jesus Christ had to give Himself in our place to receive punishment for sin, to reconcile us with God. The Holy Spirit must renew our spirits before we can begin to build the kingdom of God. The salvation that Christ purchased for us includes more than going to heaven when we die; it includes the restoration of all the negative effects of the Fall, to "unite all things" (Ephesians 1:7-10), to "reconcile" all things (Colossians 1:19-20).

Jesus is the Lord of everything. There is no aspect of life, and no area of thought, that is outside of His territory. As Christians, we desire to see Him glorified in everything.

A few years ago, my wife and I visited Barcelona, Spain, and had the privilege of seeing the *Sagrada Familia* cathedral, which had been planned by Antoni Gaudí at the end of the 19th century, but is still under construction. I've never seen anything like it. High steeples reach toward God with crosses and colorful fruit. Nature's geometry is mingled with the architecture, and Bible scenes are sculptured every place you look. Light is drawn into the sanctuary from above through cone shaped openings. It has made me think about our task as Christians: we are to bring the light of heaven into this world, and we are to offer up spiritual fruit in thanksgiving to God.

How to Develop a Christian Worldview

I will be using the term "Christian worldview" in the sense of *a mentality formed of biblical principles to think about all areas of life*. It means thinking in a Christian way about everything. We could call it a *biblical mindset*. To use an illustration of Calvin, it means putting on Christian "eyeglasses" to see the world.[15]

James Sire uses the term to refer to our most basic beliefs. For him, the Christian worldview includes important doctrines such as the existence of a personal God who created the world, the fact that man is made in God's image, the Fall and redemption.[16] Albert Wolters focuses on the themes of creation, Fall, and redemption.[17] These are essential aspects of our "eyeglasses," and often such beliefs are what people have in mind when they speak of a Christian worldview. In this book, I will also focus in the first chapters on some basic issues, such as our view of truth, our view of how to relate to culture, and a comparison of Christianity with non-Christian worldviews, making suggestions for defending the Christian view. However, in the last half of the book I will focus on some examples of how to use those eyeglasses to see the world.

---

[15] John Calvin used the illustration of the Bible as eyeglasses to interpret creation in the *Institutes*, Book I, Chapter 6, Paragraph 1.

[16] James W. Sire, *The Universe Next Door* (Downers Grove, IL: InterVarsity Press, 1997).

[17] Albert M. Wolters, *Creation Regained; Biblical Basics for a Reformational Worldview*, second edition (Grand Rapids: Eerdmans, 2008) Kindle edition. This book was written as an introduction to the philosophy of D. H. T. Vollenhoven and H. Dooyeweerd for a Christian Philosophy course at the *Toronto Institute for Christian Studies* (p. 131).

1. The Christian Concept of the Truth

A Christian worldview presupposes a Christian concept of the truth. We will look at this more in the next chapter, but it's important to mention a few points here:

-Truth is not relative, but absolute. It is not different for different people. It does not change from one day to another. It continues to be the truth, whether we understand it or not, and whether we believe it or not.

-It's not subjective, but objective. It does not depend on my mind, but rather on the mind of God. It is not within me, but within God.

-It's not independent of God; all truth comes from the mind of God.

-The truth does not come as disconnected independent "loose" pieces. Everything is interconnected and interdependent as a package.

-I can't know the truth without God's help. Truth is not something that man finds on his own. If God doesn't reveal it to me, I will never know it.

-It is not inclusive, but exclusive. It's not dialectical but antithetical. Whatever is not in agreement with the mind of God is *false* and cannot be mixed with the truth. Truth is not a "soup" in which more ingredients make the flavor better. It's rather a perfect "filet" steak.

-Truth does not evolve; it's eternal. "Newer" things are not necessarily better in this case. Anything true has already been thought by God Himself.

-The truth is revealed to man in the Bible and in creation. The two sources don't contradict each other.

-To think correctly, we should "think God's thoughts after Him" (Cornelius Van Til)[18], and to think God's thoughts, we need to think in agreement with the Bible.

2. The Use of the Bible in Developing a Christian Worldview

The Bible gives us the presuppositions, the guidelines, for studying everything. It adjusts our lenses to see the world more clearly. We might not always find specific Bible passages that deal directly with our topic of study, but biblical principles will always give us a foundation.

Science   **Economics**

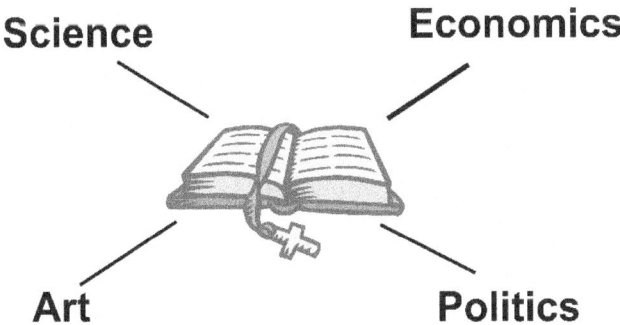

Art   **Politics**

---

[18] Cornelius Van Til, *Nature and Scripture*, p. 278, also in *Common Grace*, p. 28, quoted by Greg Bahnsen in *Van Til's Apologetic* (Phillipsburg, New Jersey: P&R, 1998), p. 225. See also *The Defense of the Faith* (Phillipsburg, New Jersey, Presbyterian and Reformed, 1979), pp. 47, 48. In another place he says that "...our notions or our concepts are finite replicas of the notions of God". (*Introduction to Systematic Theology*, quoted in *Jerusalem and Athens*, Presbyterian and Reformed, 1971, p. 325).

3. The Relation between Christian Worldview and Other Areas of Study

Courses on Christian worldview are often taught in seminaries and other Christian institutions, but it's hard to know where they fit in the program. For a liberal arts program, it would easily serve as an introduction to the rest of the courses. In a typical seminary program, it's not so easy. Seminary subjects overlap in many ways, but each has its own emphasis.

1) Systematic theology studies the Bible in order to systematize its teaching about topics such as God, man, and salvation. It seeks to answer questions by arranging and harmonizing the teachings of Scripture on the particular subject.
2) Biblical theology studies biblical themes in the order of the history of revelation and in the context of the plan of redemption. For example, it may study the theme of the development of the kingdom of God, or it might study the different ways in which God reveals Himself in different periods of history.
3) Historical theology studies the history of the development of doctrines. For example, it may study how the Church came to understand the doctrine of the Trinity.
4) Apologetics studies the defense of the Christian faith in response to non-Christian challenges.
5) Christian worldview takes biblical guidelines to study themes related to culture, the sciences, humanities, and the arts.

Systematic theology and biblical theology concentrate more on the Bible itself, while historical theology focuses on history and apologetics dialogues with non-Christian philosophy. Christian worldview uses biblical principles to study other issues in the world outside of the Bible. Christian worldview is sometimes grouped with apologetics, and it does involve relating our faith to an unbelieving world, but it is really a unique subject.

The Bible doesn't always give us detailed answers regarding some issues that we study in a course on Christian Worldview. We examine complex topics that involve numerous factors, making some things seem blurry at times. The Bible still serves as our glasses, but some things seem farther away and are not always easy to see clearly.

For example, the Bible does not tell us exactly how to run the economy or the government of a particular country, but it gives us some guidelines about material possessions, about good stewardship, and about the task and authority of the government. The Scriptures provide orientation, but we need to apply the principles in our unique context. This means that there will be more "gray" areas in Christian worldview than in systematic theology, and that we should be more tolerant with our fellow Christians who might not agree with us completely in some areas.

4. How to Do It

The prerequisites: To develop a Christian worldview, we first need to know the Scriptures. The Bible is the main source of our convictions. However, we also need to know the world in which we live. The process of cultivating a Christian worldview is related to everything around us: the government, the arts, the supermarket, and the schools. Finally, we should be familiar with the thoughts of others on the subject, both Christian and secular. It requires a continual dialogue with others.

Steps:

a. Ask yourself questions. Cultivate your curiosity. Begin with some concern. Without questions, you won't find answers. For example, you could ask, "Is abortion ever permissible?" Or maybe, "How should we respond to the LGBTQ movement?"

b. Examine the biblical teachings. Research what the Bible says about the issue. You may not find passages that answer your question directly, but they should give you some general principles.

c. Research other sources. Study related materials, by non-Christians as well as Christians. You might also be able to do your own research, such as surveys or experiments.

d. Examine the Bible again. After investigating the ideas of others, go back to the Bible again. The other writings will probably help you see new things in the Scriptures or help you see the same passages in a new light.

e. Meditate and reflect. Ask the Lord to guide your thought process and give you wisdom.

f. Draw your conclusions. You may modify them over the years, but make your best effort to develop a Christian perspective and live according to your convictions.

This is a continual process of analysis, and it might not be done in this exact order. Our reflection revolves around both the world and the Bible. The more we know the Bible, the better we understand the world, and the more we know the world, the better we understand the Bible. The good thing about this adventure is that we are always discovering new things! We are like mountain climbers: the higher we climb, the better the view.

Our Testimony

There was a movie called "A Beautiful Mind," that serves as an excellent illustration of the non-believer's situation. It's based on the life of John Nash, a mathematical genius who received the Nobel Prize for his new theory related to economics. He suffered from schizophrenia, seeing people that didn't exist. (In real life, he didn't see them, but only heard their voices.) Desiring to do something important, he imagined that he was helping the government of the United States to decipher Russian codes and to find messages about spying activities. Among the people that he imagined was a young girl about ten years old. One day Nash discovered an important inconsistency in his imaginary world: years had gone by, but the girl still seemed to be the same age! This detail helped him realize that the imaginary world was not real. It was the beginning of a healing process. The nonbeliever has a similar problem. I am not saying that he is mentally ill, but that he is trying to live according to convictions that don't coincide with the world God has created, with the truths God has revealed, or with the instincts that God has put in his heart and mind.

John Nash's wife is an example to us, because she played a key role in his process of healing. She loved him and helped him, despite the difficulties. She was always at his side, living a "normal" life, and did not abandon him even in his worst moments. This should be our role among non-believers. We should love them and stay beside them, trying to be consistent, even when they are inconsistent. Let them see the coherency between our life and thought, in contrast with their own confusion and uncertainty. Intellectual integrity and harmony between our thoughts and our lives are fundamental aspects of our testimony.

Review Questions

1. In what sense do we as Evangelicals suffer from "intellectual schizophrenia"?
2. In what sense do many comments about current events reflect "consequentialism"?
3. Mention causes of intellectual inconsistency.
4. What does Blamires mean when he says there is no "Christian mind"?
5. Mention the first two passages quoted in the chapter to challenge us to develop a Christian worldview.
6. What is the "cultural mandate"?
7. What does salvation include, according to Ephesians 1:7-10 and Colossians 1:19-20?
8. What is a "Christian worldview"?
9. How do we use the Bible to develop a Christian worldview?
10. What is the difference between Christian worldview and other branches of theology?
11. What are the steps of developing a Christian perspective on an issue?
12. In what sense is John Nash an illustration of the non-believer?
13. In what sense is the wife of John Nash an example for us?

Questions for reflection
1. How do you see "intellectual schizophrenia" among Christians in your context?
2. What areas of thought and study do you have more difficulty harmonizing with your Christian faith?

CHAPTER 2
THE WAR FOR THE TRUTH [19]

Most of us have lived our whole lives under a persistent cloud of anxiety due to the possibility of a nuclear war that could destroy most of the world. Os Guinness calls the twentieth century "the world's most murderous century," and asserts that 100 million were killed in war, another 100 million because of political repression, and another 100 million in "ethnic and sectarian violence."[20] This violence obviously concerns me deeply.

Nevertheless, I am even more concerned about another war, less visible, but more dangerous. It's the war of ideas. It's the war about truth and the source of the truth. Sometimes it's even a war against the very existence of truth itself. The New Testament declares that our real struggle is not against flesh and blood, but against principalities and powers, rulers of darkness and spiritual hosts (Ephesians 6:12). Paul exhorts us to be prepared for this battle by putting on the "belt of truth" (Ephesians 6:14).

Kenneth Myers highlights a change that has occurred with the dominant role of television during the last generations. We could include movies, computers, smart phones and tablets. The change is that communication has become more visual and less verbal. Images communicate "immediately and intuitively," while words communicate in "linear, logical form." The problem is that some things can't be communicated just with images. Furthermore,

[19] This chapter is a modified version of a talk presented by the author to the *Second Congress of Evangelical Teachers* in Valparaíso, Chile, July 19, 2002.
[20] Os Guinness, *The Case for Civility* (New York: HarperCollins, 2008), p. 2.

communication with words can be judged more easily to be true or false.[21] This also means that, even though people often trust what they see in images more than what they read, images can in fact deceive us more easily.

The Internet and social media provide platforms to easily promote false ideas and distorted information, especially with the increased capabilities of Artificial Intelligence. The truth becomes what the multitudes seem to accept as valid, or simply whatever I want to believe. Internet search engines can lead a person to become more and more enclosed in a certain view of something, even though it might be wrong, without the person realizing it. People can easily become confused, even lose hope in being sure about anything.

Before we talk in later chapters about what we believe, we need to start with even more basic questions: Can we be sure of knowing the truth? If so, how? This study is called epistemology. First, we'll briefly analyze the background of contemporary philosophical thought, focusing especially on the concept of truth. Then we'll identify the inconsistencies in the non-Christian views of truth and defend the Christian view. We need to be "prepared to make a defense to anyone who asks you for a reason for the hope that is in you..." (1 Peter 3:15).

The Two Francis Bacons

During what some call the modern age (starting in the 16th century), the tendency was to trust reason and science. For example, the philosopher Francis Bacon (1561-1626), was an empiricist. He believed that the world was orderly and

---

[21] Kenneth A. Myers, *All God's Children and Blue Suede Shoes* (Wheaton, IL: Crossway, 1989), pp. 162-163.

that you could understand it and discover the truth through inductive logic and the scientific method.

However, in our day, many have lost interest and confidence in this method. In *Modern Times*, Paul Johnson suggests that *uncertainty* is the attitude that characterizes mankind since early in the twentieth century. He explains that the theory of relativity of Einstein, the instability of the international situation, and the declaration of Nietzsche that "God is dead" have caused people to live in a "world without direction and at the mercy of a relativistic universe."[22]

There is a painting by another more recent Francis Bacon called "Head VI" (1949), which expresses the terror of uncertainty in contemporary humanity. It shows a man dressed in religious garb, seated within a glass cube as if he were in an exhibition. His head is disappearing from the nose and above, showing only black shadows. The only part of his head that you can see clearly is his mouth, open in a spine-tingling scream. Curiously, this painting reflects a reaction to the philosophy held by the philosopher of the same name centuries before.[23]

What happened between the first Francis Bacon and the second? Modernism was replaced by Postmodernism. Trust in reason and science was replaced with uncertainty. People realized that, if the modern philosophers were right, then mankind has lost its dignity and meaning. If everything is a result of an impersonal process, as these philosophers had proposed, then to be consistent, they must admit that their own thoughts are also part of that impersonal process, and

---

[22] Paul Johnson, *Tiempos modernos* (Buenos Aires: Javier Vergara Editor, 1988), p. 59. Translated by the author from Spanish.

[23] This painting was apparently inspired by a painting of Pope Innocent X by Velásquez.
See Wikipedia article on Bacon, including comments on this picture, at: http://en.wikipedia.org/wiki/Francis_Bacon_(painter) (April 19, 2010).

Intellectual Integrity

therefore that they can't be trusted. Bacon, the 20th century painter, once wrote, "Man is aware that he is an accident, that he is a completely futile being, and that he must finish the game without reason."[24] It's not surprising that some people identify with the frightened man closed in the box in Bacon's painting.

The Line of Uncertainty

Francis Schaeffer talks about a "line of despair" in modern thought in his book, *The God Who is There*. [25] He points out key thinkers and artists who cross over this threshold and stop trying to make sense of things. I would like to go beyond this moment, both in modern philosophy and Greek philosophy, to see the larger historical pattern. I believe that there is a general tendency of philosophers to struggle with uncertainty.

You can observe what I call a "line of uncertainty" in western philosophy. Basically, it's a vacillation between certainty and uncertainty.[26]

---

[24] H. R. Rookmaaker, *Modern Art and the Death of a Culture* (Downers Grove, IL: InterVarsity Press, 1970), p. 174.

[25] Francis Schaeffer, *The God Who is There* (Downers Grove, Illinois: InterVarsity Press, 1968), p.21.

[26] For a more complete development of this study of philosophy and the "line of uncertainty," see the author's book, *The Certainty of the Faith; Apologetics in an Uncertain World* (Phillipsburg, N.J.: P&R Publishing, 2007).

Certainty

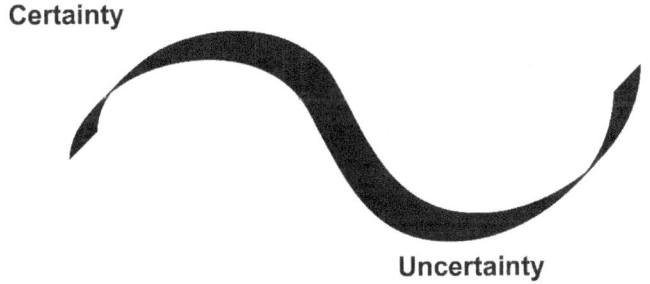

Uncertainty

But it's more complicated than this. They seem to pass through five stages: 1) They start with certainty of knowing the truth, 2) then they doubt and 3) fall into despair, losing all certainty, 4) struggle to overcome the despair and uncertainty, and 5) finally begin focusing on ethics, while remaining skeptical of ever finding certainty. I think many people follow a similar pattern in their personal spiritual pilgrimage.

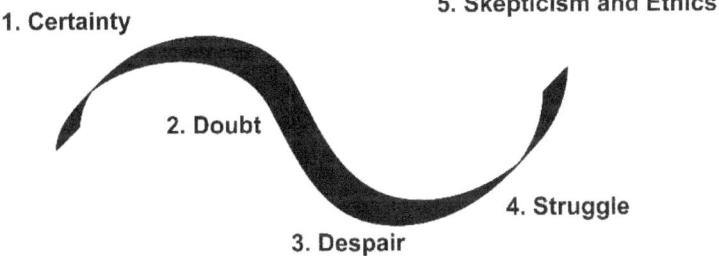

When Schaeffer speaks of a "line of despair," he is referring to what would be the specific point on this "line of uncertainty" when they cross over from stage 2 to stage 3.

1. Certainty

5. Skepticism and Ethics

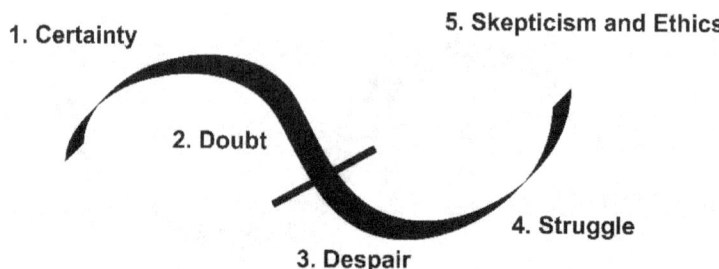

2. Doubt

4. Struggle

3. Despair

Let's begin with the Greeks, giving a simplified review of the basic tendencies. Thales thought that he could discover basic reality behind everything; he thought it was water (stage 1). But Heraclitus observed that everything was constantly changing, that "you cannot bathe twice in the same river" because when you step back into the river, the water you were in before has already passed by. Protagoras agrees with Heraclitus and proposes that truth is relative, that "man is the measure of all things" (stage 2).[27] Gorgias concluded that, if everything changes, you can't be sure of anything or communicate anything. In the moment you believe something, it has already changed. Cratylus, being consistent with this view, simply stopped talking (stage 3)!

The next stage brings us the giants of Greek philosophy who struggle to rescue the hope of knowing the truth. While Socrates stated that "I only know that I know nothing," this was only the starting point for him. He believed that in dialogue with others, we can discover the truth. Plato, in his allegory of the cave, suggested that we can discover the truth by way of mystical experience. He believed that our souls existed before inhabiting our bodies, and that our souls can remember the truth. Aristotle put his hope in logic (stage 4).

---

[27] Frederick Copleston, *A History of Philosophy*, vol. I (Garden City, New York: Image Books, 1962), p 110.

But as John Frame explains, neither Plato nor Aristotle can explain fundamental things such change, motion and ethics. He asserts that the changing world for Plato is "irrational," and the "Prime Mover" of Aristotle is "contentless and abstract."[28] Finally, the next stage of Greek philosophy is dominated by the Skeptics, as well as the Stoics and Epicureans who emphasized ethics. Notice that they could not live with uncertainty and despair, struggling anxiously to find the truth. Notice also that people can't stop talking about ethics, even though they may be uncertain of the truth (stage 5).

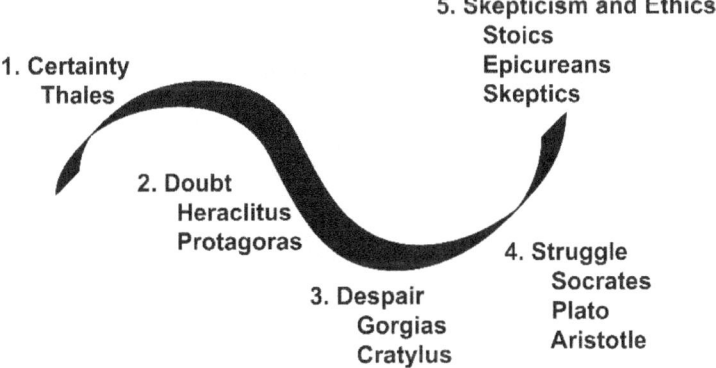

A similar pattern appears in modern philosophy. Christian theology had been dominant during the Middle Ages, then thinking became secular. Special revelation in the Scriptures no longer was regarded as the primary source of truth, and man replaced God as the center of attention. In stage one of the modern age, we find Sir Francis Bacon (1561-1626) who believes in the scientific method),

---

[28] John Frame, *A History of Western Philosophy and Theology* (Phillipsburg, NJ: P&R Publishing, 2015), pp. 69, 77.

Descartes (1596-165) who believes in rationalism ("I think, therefore I am"), and Locke (1632-1704) who is an empiricist (what you see is what you know). In different ways, they all trust their capacity to know the truth. In stage two, Hume (1711-1776) is also an empiricist, but skeptical about finding the truth (we can't even be sure the sun will rise tomorrow).

In stage three, Marquis de Sade and Nietzsche cross over into despair and a loss of absolute truth and ethical norms. Marquis de Sade (1740-1814), is known for his libertinism and his pleasure in sexual cruelty, from whence comes the name "sadism." Cynical and dedicated to his vices, he was not concerned about the consequences of his actions. He wrote:

> By Nature created, created with very keen tastes, with very strong passions; placed on this earth for the sole purpose of yielding to them and satisfying them ... [29]

Nietzsche (1844-1900) also represents the low point of despair. However, he is not exactly in the same place *chronologically* as Sade; he came after Kant and Hegel. He speaks of the "death" of God, leading us to think that nothing makes sense (nihilism) and that there is no objective basis for morality. He suggests that Christianity encourages weakness, and that we should become like the *Ubermensch* (superman), who has been freed from external ethical norms and can create his own values, imposing his own will on others. Not only can the *Ubermensch* suffer, but he can also make others suffer without feeling bad about it. This view apparently

---

[29] Marquis de Sade, "Dialogue between a Priest and a Dying Man," *Justine, Philosophy in the Bedroom, and Other Writings*, trans. Austryn Wainhouse and Richard Seaver (Jackson, TN: Grove Press, 1994), 165–66, 174.

influenced tyrants such as Hitler, Mussolini and Stalin. In both Marquis de Sade and Nietzsche, we look down into the dark abyss of moral cruelty that can be the product of despair.

In stage four, Kant and Hegel try to save the possibility of knowing the truth and to avoid falling into despair. (Even so, Nietzsche dared to go back and look into the darkness.) Kant proposed that knowledge comes from a combination of perception and a mental process imposed on the raw material that passes through our mind. But he realized that this does not leave room for freedom and can't explain things like morality. So he made a distinction between a realm in which "pure reason" functions and a realm in which "practical reason" functions. The problem is that this second area is foggy and unknowable.[30]

Hegel developed the concept of the dialectic, in which ideas evolve over history as guided by a great spirit. Instead of looking at two apparently contradictory positions (a thesis and its antithesis) as mutually exclusive choices, we should look at them as distinct aspects of a larger truth and expect them to merge into a synthesis. The problem with this view is that it leaves you without absolute unchanging truth and leaves you uncertain about knowing anything for sure.[31]

Existentialists such as Jean Paul Sartre and Albert Camus, coming after Nietzsche, struggled to avoid the consequences of nihilism. Camus said, "In the darkest depths of our nihilism I have sought only for the means to transcend

---

[30] Immanuel Kant, *Critique of Pure Reason*, trans. J. M. D. Meiklejohn (New York: Prometheus Books, 1990), 21–45, 93. John Frame, *A History of Western Philosophy and Theology*, 264-270.

[31] John Frame, *A History of Western Philosophy and Theology*, 270-277.

Intellectual Integrity

nihilism."[32] While life seems absurd, man can determine his own meaning. But this is subjective and doesn't really solve the problem of uncertainty.

In stage five, liberal theologians lost the basis for absolute truth when they lost their trust in the infallible Scriptures, but they still talk a lot about ethics. *Liberation* theologians (a particular school of *liberal* theology) emphasize ethics (justice for the poor and oppressed), while admitting uncertainty.

José Míguez Bonino is a Protestant representative of liberation theology. He accepts a concept of communication that eliminates all certainty.[33] No one can be sure that they have communicated something correctly or understood something correctly. This reminds us of Gorgias! For Bonino, this problem also affects the communication between God and man; it's impossible to be sure that you have understood God. Bonino encouraged Christians to commit to the revolutionary Marxist movement to help the poor and oppressed, but he admitted that this commitment was an "uncertain alliance," [una alianza inquietante] and that liberation theology could be wrong.

> It is simply an initial and ambiguous answer and a tenuous perception of a new task and a new responsibility. It is destined to die. May God permit that its life and death be fruitful.[34]

---

[32] Albert Camus, *L'Été*, quoted in James W. Sire, *The Universe Next Door* (Downers Grove, IL: InterVarsity Press, 1997), p. 95.

[33] José Míguez Bonino, *La fe en busca de eficacia* [Faith in search of efficacy.] (Salamanca: Ediciones Sígueme, 1977) pp. 118, 119.

[34] José Míguez Bonino, "New Trends in Theology", Duke Divinity School Review 42 (Fall, 1997): 141,142.

Finally, postmodernists also reject the notion of absolute truth, and although they say they don't believe in ethical norms, they seek happiness, much like the Epicureans, and they insist on tolerance. In that sense, they do show a definite ethical emphasis, although not in the traditional manner.

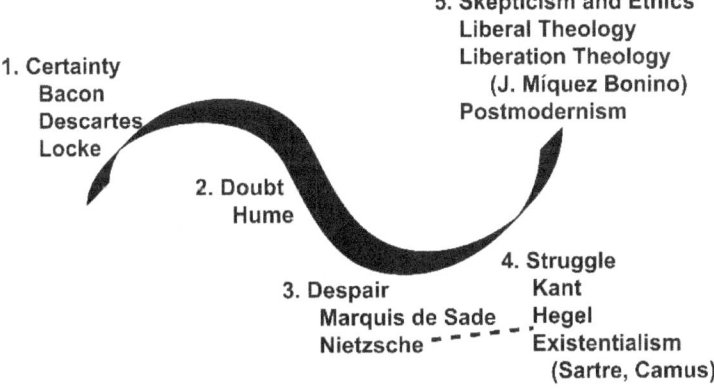

5. Skepticism and Ethics
Liberal Theology
Liberation Theology
(J. Míquez Bonino)
Postmodernism

1. Certainty
Bacon
Descartes
Locke

2. Doubt
Hume

4. Struggle
Kant
3. Despair
Marquis de Sade — **Hegel**
Nietzsche **Existentialism**
(Sartre, Camus)

Many individuals who are seeking the truth without Christ also go through a similar cycle of certainty, doubt, despair, and struggle, often ending with a skeptical view of truth combined with an emphasis on ethics. Curiously, sometimes a person who rejects the possibility of knowing the truth is the most adamant about certain ethical issues.

Not all non-Christians today are postmodernists. In fact, some consider that postmodernism as a movement has faded.[35] Many people still believe in science, as evidenced by the popularity of the book by Stephen Hawking and Leonard

---

[35] See the reference to Donald A. Carson, *Christ and Culture* in the preface of this book.

Mlodinow, *The Grand Design*.[36] Others simply don't care. Still, the tendency over the last century has been one of uncertainty.

The only good thing about this contemporary uncertainty is that it provides an excellent opportunity to speak of the gospel and the Word of God. We have a message of hope and certainty in this confused world.

Problems with Non-Christian Concepts of Truth

Soon after giving my life to Christ, I encountered many people who made me doubt the Bible. While living with this uncertainty, I realized that if I didn't believe the Bible, I couldn't really be sure about *anything!* I wanted to believe it, but could not justify it in my own mind.

I went to seminary in search of answers. Thankfully, I had the privilege of taking classes with Cornelius Van Til, who I consider one of the greatest apologists of the twentieth century. It was his simple exposition of the story of Adam and Eve that convicted me of my problem. He explained that, when God told them they would die if they ate from the Tree of the Knowledge of Good and Evil, they responded in an illegitimate way. As they questioned, "I wonder...., I wonder.... who is right?", they were arrogantly pretending to be able to find the truth by themselves, independent of God. In fact, they were setting themselves up as judges over God. This is man's basic problem in seeking the truth. Who are we, creatures of God, to question Him?

When I read this, it pierced my heart. I realized I was doing the very same thing when I questioned God's Word in the Scriptures. I was putting myself as judge over God. I

---

[36] Stephen Hawking and Leonard Mlodinow, The Grand Design (New York: Bantam, 2010).

Intellectual Integrity

asked Him to forgive me and stopped doubting. God became my source of all truth. I thought, "If God says the moon is made of green cheese, then I will change my idea of the moon and of green and of cheese! If God says it, it's true!" Of course, God will never make a statement that so clearly contradicts our normal use of language, reason, and observation, but this idea expressed my new attitude of absolute submission to Him.

This is the point I want to highlight: It is not just because God is so intelligent that He knows the truth. God *invents* the truth! When God thinks something, it is true *simply because He thinks it*!

The problem of man in seeking the truth is basically that he pretends to be the judge. Consciously or not, he sets himself up as the one who decides what the truth is, when in reality he is only a dependent creature who must receive the truth from God.

When he thinks he has a right to decide what the truth is, he has two basic choices about how he proceeds: He may assume that truth is outside of himself, or that truth is inside his head, that truth is objective or that it is subjective.

If Truth is Objective

If he thinks truth is objective, outside himself, he can't be sure he is perceiving things correctly. He also encounters the dilemma of needing to know everything to be sure of anything. This is because there are an infinite number of "facts" out there, and tomorrow he may discover a new fact that makes him change his mind about something he believes today.

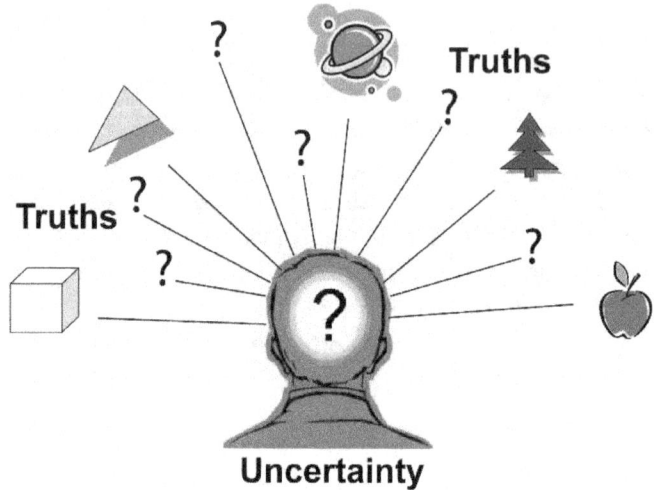

When talking to someone who holds such a view, we can ask a question we know he can't answer. Even a simple apple presents us with many unknown facts: How many apples were on the same tree from which this apple was picked? Will there be apples on the earth in 2,000 years? Are there apples somewhere else in the universe? The questions are valid, but most people know they can't answer them. This highlights the problem of uncertainty. We can humbly suggest that there are many things he doesn't know and ask how he can be sure there aren't some important truths that would completely change his perspective.

If Truth is Subjective

If he thinks truth is subjective, in his own mind, he might be able to defend his view philosophically. He simply decides what is true for him. But eventually he will have to admit that he can't live consistently with this in the real world. There is a world outside his mind that he can't control. He knows that he doesn't really decide what is true.

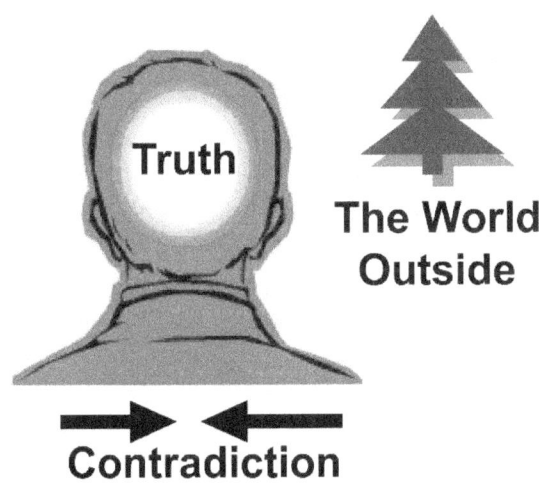

If we talk to someone who takes this position, we could ask him to imagine that we are at the railroad tracks and he is standing right in the middle between the rails. I would ask him what he would do if he saw a train coming. Could he simply decide that the train is not coming? I am sure he wouldn't try it! He would jump off the tracks just like anybody else in his right mind! What does this prove? Simply that he cannot live consistently with the idea that his own mind determines the truth.

If Truth is Impossible

These problems might lead some to deny the possibility of knowledge altogether. However, in the moment they affirm that nothing can be affirmed, they have contradicted themselves. If I can't be sure of anything, how can I be sure that I can't be sure of anything? Again, we come back to Cratylus; it would be better to say nothing!

While I was studying in seminary, I worked as a night supervisor in a college library nearby to pay for my studies. There was a student who worked there also and frequently talked with me about my faith. She once said, "You can't be sure of anything." When I asked her how she could be sure of that, she became furious and stomped out. Several hours later she returned and blurted, "I *think* that you can't be sure of anything." She abruptly turned around and walked away without waiting for an answer. At least she had become aware of her inconsistency.

If Anything is True

The same problems may lead others to affirm that *anything* can be true. Have you ever heard someone say, "What is true for you is true for you, and what is true for me is true for me"? In our day it's popular to avoid conflict, and in the name of tolerance, accept everything. But if everything is true, then being true loses its meaning!

We would be like the young man who appeared before his church leaders to be examined for ordination to be a pastor. When they asked him if he believed in the divinity of Jesus, he said, "I don't deny the divinity of Jesus; I don't deny the divinity of anybody!" The problem is, if everybody is divine, then divinity loses its meaning. The very concept of divinity includes being superior to everyone else. If everybody is God, then nobody is God.

Truths contain within themselves the denial of other points of view. For example, if we say there is only *one* straight line between two points, then we are denying that there are *two* straight lines between two points. We can't

Intellectual Integrity

believe both. If we say that "A" is true and that "A" is also not true, then we have abandoned normal reasonable communication and normal rational thinking.

The Biblical Concept of Truth

1. We depend on God to know the truth.

The biblical concept of the truth is not centered on man, but on God. Man does not discover the truth on his own. God knows all truth, in fact He is the creator of all truth, and He chooses to reveal some truth to us.

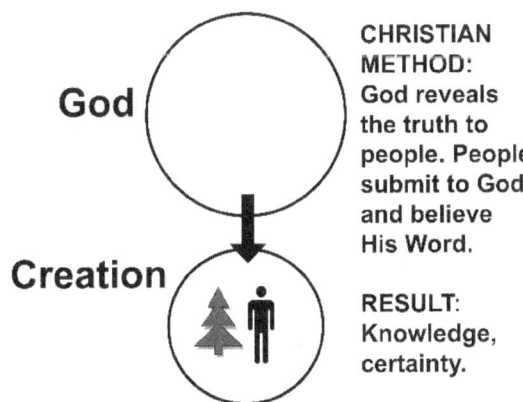

God

CHRISTIAN METHOD: God reveals the truth to people. People submit to God and believe His Word.

Creation

RESULT: Knowledge, certainty.

He promises that we can know the truth by listening to Him and believing Him. Despite the problems of interpretation, human weakness, and a multitude of factors present in any context, God Himself assures us that he will let us know the truth. It depends on Him, not on us. As Francis Schaeffer expressed it, we can know the truth *truly*, but not *exhaustively*.[37]

---

[37] Francis Schaeffer, *The God Who is There*, pp. 32-33.

Knowing the truth is not only an intellectual process. Of course, it includes an intellectual acceptance of the verbal propositions that God gives us, but it is not only intellectual because it involves a personal trust in God, as well as a willingness to submit to God. Someone has said that truth is like a virtuous woman who undresses only in the context of a relationship of marriage and fidelity. If we are not faithful disciples, we will not learn the truth.

John 8:31, 32
So Jesus said to the Jews who had believed in him, "If you abide in my word, you are truly my disciples, and you will know the truth, and the truth will set you free."

2. We should take every thought captive to Christ.
One of the consequences of the biblical concept of truth is that all truth is related to Christ. Jesus is "the way, the truth, and the life" (John 14:6). When Jesus became man, He revealed what God is like. He explained the truth about life, about our origins, about our future, about the Father and the Holy Spirit. Since the purpose of history is salvation in Christ, every event is related to Him somehow. Part of our task in studying history and in investigating the creation is to seek Christ and His glory.

2 Corinthians 10:5
We destroy arguments and every lofty opinion raised against the knowledge of God, and take every thought captive to obey Christ.

3. God reveals His truth both in creation and in Scripture.
God created nature with a message engraved in every detail. The stars reveal His glory, the mountains remind us of

His majesty, and the ocean tells us of the depth of His grace. As Van Til said in his classes, all of creation has God's "fingerprints" on it.

Romans 1:20
For his invisible attributes, namely, his eternal power and divine nature, have been clearly perceived, ever since the creation of the world, in the things that have been made. So they are without excuse.

Just as a painting communicates something of the artist, nature tells us about God. But we need help to interpret creation properly. The Bible is our divine code for this task. There is no contradiction between the Bible and creation.

Philip Yancey refers to an illustration of G. K. Chesterton, who says that man is like a survivor from a shipwreck. Yancey imagines that a man wakes up surrounded by objects from the ship in which he was a passenger: coins, a compass, and clothes. These objects indicate something about the world from which he came, but he needs help to understand what has happened.[38] In the same way, creation gives us signs about God and about life before the Fall, but we need further explanation. I would add that finding the Bible is like finding the captain's diary. The Bible not only explains the tragedy we have experienced, but it also tells us how we can be rescued.

Francis Schaeffer helps us with another illustration of a torn book found in the attic.

---

[38] Philip Yancey, *Soul Survivor; How My Soul Survived the Church* (New York: Doubleday, 2001), pp. 51-52. He refers to G. K. Chesterton in *Orthodoxy*. See Kindle edition, p. 52. <www.deaddodopublishing.co.uk, 2018>.

Imagine a book which has been mutilated, leaving just one inch of printed matter on each page. Although it would obviously be impossible to piece together and understand the book's story, yet few people would imagine that what had been left had come together by chance. However, if the torn parts of each page were found in the attic and were added in the right places, then the story could be read and would make sense.

So it is with Christianity: the ripped pages remaining in the book correspond to the abnormal universe and the abnormal man we have now. The parts of the pages which are discovered correspond to the Scriptures which are God's propositional communication to mankind, which not only touch 'religious' truth but also touch the cosmos and history which are open to verification. [39]

4. All areas of study are related to the Bible.

We need the Bible to understand any aspect of creation. This means that every area of study, whether it is science, linguistics, history, or art, must be evaluated in the light of Scripture. We need to put on Christian glasses to study any aspect of life or creation. For example, when we study linguistics, we find that the biblical account of the Tower of Babel explains the origin of languages. Different languages did not simply evolve gradually over time from one mother tongue. When we study art, we should consider the fact that man is creative because he is the image of God. As we study science, we can point to the marvelous beauty of God's

---

[39] Francis Schaeffer, *The God Who is There* (Downers Grove, Illinois: InterVarsity Press, 1998), pp. 137-138 (p. 108 in the first edition of 1968).

creation. For history, we can refer to the facts recorded in the Bible, and we can see God as the ultimate author of history, interpreting all events under His sovereign guiding hand.

You might ask, "What does the Bible have to do with something like mathematics?" My brother was a university math professor most of his life. He argues that math is one area of study that is basically consistent with a Christian worldview. According to him, when a Christian does math, he is being more consistent than a non-Christian when he does it. For example, if a non-Christian believes the world is disorderly and that it came to exist through a process guided by chance, then he would have no reason to expect math to apply to the real world. He also tells me that on higher levels of study, mathematics becomes philosophical.

Vern Poythress, professor of theology at *Westminster Theological Seminary*, who has doctorates in both math and theology, has written about the differences between the way Christians view math and the way non-Christians view it. As an example, he speaks of the value of "π" (*pi*). This value is used in geometry for things like calculating the area of a circle ($A = \pi r^2$). However, it is a value that we cannot calculate exactly; the decimals continue infinitely (3.141592...). There is an Internet site designed to exhibit the calculation of the value of π, in which a series of numbers continue to cross the screen endlessly. The question is, does π really exist? Some mathematicians say no, because we cannot know the value. Others say yes. A Christian can accept the existence of something that man can't calculate, because he knows that God knows the value.[40] If

---

[40] Vern Poythress, "A Biblical View of Mathematics" in *Foundations of Christian Scholarship; Essays in the Van Til Perspective*] (Vallecito, California: Ross House Books, 1976), pp. 159-190.

mathematics leads us back to God and His Word, then everything does too!

5. The truth should be lived.

    Although I do not share their basic viewpoints, I believe that liberation theologians have reminded us of an important aspect of the truth: to really know something means also to live it. José Míguez Bonino makes a valid criticism of traditional western theology for being too abstract and theoretical, unattached from reality. He says it is "without conflict and tension, hovering over history and the world,"[41] and that it is "introverted."[42] He thinks that the traditional concept of truth has received a lot of influence from Platonic idealism. This concept separates truth from action. It supposes that one can know the truth by simply formulating the concepts correctly in his mind. Whether he lives according to these concepts or not does not affect his "knowledge." The only important thing is that his concept corresponds precisely with "reality."

        In this perspective, the truth belongs to a "universe of truth," complete in itself, that may be more or less faithfully reproduced or copied in correct "propositions," in a theory (a contemplation of that universe) that corresponds to that truth. Then, as a second step, there is an "application" of that theory in a particular historical situation. The truth thus exists before its historical effect, and is independent of it. Its validity or legitimacy must be

---

[41] José Míguez Bonino, "Comments on "Unity of the Church- Unity of Mankind"", *Ecumenical Review* 24 (January, 1972): 48.
[42] José Míguez Bonino, "The Struggle of the Poor and the Church", *Ecumenical Review* 27 (January, 1975): 38.

Intellectual Integrity

confirmed in relation with that "abstract heaven of truth," totally apart from its historical appearance. It is this concept of truth that has caused a crisis in Latin American theology.[43]

Míguez Bonino insists that, according to the Bible, to know the truth is to live it. Knowledge of the truth cannot be separated from obedience. Quoting John 7:17, "If anyone is willing to do His will, he will know of the teaching, whether it is of God or whether I speak from Myself," he argues that if our heart is not willing to obey, God does not permit us to understand the truth, even in an intellectual way. He also argues that biblically, to know God means to have a faithful personal relationship with Him.[44] [45]

I agree with Míguez Bonino in this warning. Possibly unconsciously, many Christians adopt an unbiblical notion of the truth. We tend to think that to know the truth means simply having an idea in our minds that corresponds to reality, as if the truth were a galaxy of propositions floating in space. But the biblical concept of truth doesn't permit us to say we really "know" something if we merely give our intellectual assent. Jesus says that if we are truly His disciples, we will know the truth, and the truth will make us free (John 8:31, 32). Knowledge of the truth brings changes in our life. James 2:17 says, "So also faith by itself, if it does not have works, is dead." To really believe something means to live according to the conviction. To "know" the truth implies faithfulness in our relationship with God.

---

[43] José Míguez Bonino, *La fe en busca de eficacia* (Salamanca: Ediciones Sígueme, 1997), pp. 113-114. Translated from Spanish by the author.

[44] José Míguez Bonino, *Christians and Marxists: The Mutual Challenge to Revolution* (Grand Rapids: Eerdmans, 1976), p. 40.

[45] José Míguez Bonino, *Ama y haz lo que quieras; hacia una ética del hombre nuevo.* (Buenos Aires: La Aurora, 1972), pp. 63-79.

Satan may "know" many biblical doctrines in his mind, but he hates God and doesn't live by these truths. Therefore, Jesus calls him the "father of lies." "When he lies, he speaks out of his own character, for he is a liar and the father of lies" (John 8:44b). Even when Satan says words that are direct quotes from the Scriptures, since he uses them to deceive, he is not speaking the "truth."

However, we also want to avoid the other extreme of affirming that the truth has nothing to do with propositions or with intellectual consent. While the truth is not *only* intellectual, it does include a cognitive aspect. In Hebrews 11:1 we read, "Now faith is the assurance of things hoped for, the *conviction* of things not seen." The heroes of the faith mentioned in this chapter acted according to their conviction that what God had said was true. Paul mentions some propositions that we must accept as an essential part of our faith, facts regarding the death and resurrection of Jesus.

1 Corinthians 15:1-5

Now I would remind you, brothers, of the gospel I preached to you, which you received, in which you stand, and by which you are being saved, if you hold fast to the word I preached to you—unless you believed in vain. For I delivered to you as of first importance what I also received: that Christ died for our sins in accordance with the Scriptures, that he was buried, that he was raised on the third day in accordance with the Scriptures, and that he appeared to Cephas, then to the twelve.

Knowing the truth is a step of faith, trusting God as the source of truth. This means we not only believe *in* God, but we believe *God*. Knowing the truth includes more than merely an intellectual acceptance of the propositions that

God reveals to us, but it certainly does not exclude it. And this brings us back to the Scriptures as our vital, supernatural connection with the mind of God himself.

6. By God's grace, non-believers can know truth.

We can only know the truth because of the grace of God. And even non-believers benefit from this grace. Although they have a truth system that doesn't recognize God as the source of truth, and although their interpretations will be different, this does not mean that they can't know any truth. Common grace, or universal grace, extends to everyone and enables them to know many things. For example, Romans 1:18-20 explains that God has revealed important things about Himself through the creation. Romans 2:15 teaches that Gentiles have God's law written on their hearts. We shouldn't underestimate God's grace working in them. John Calvin says:

> Whenever we come upon these matters in secular writers, let that admirable light of truth shining in them teach us that the mind of man, though fallen and perverted from its wholeness, is nevertheless clothed and ornamented with God's excellent gifts. If we regard the Spirit of God as the sole fountain of truth, we shall neither reject the truth itself, nor despise it wherever it shall appear, unless we wish to dishonor the Spirit of God. For by holding the gifts of the Spirit in slight esteem, we condemn and reproach the Spirit himself.[46]

---

[46] John Calvin, *Institutes of the Christian Religion*, ed. John T. McNeill. (Philadelphia: Westminster Press, 1967), Book II, Chapter 2, Section 15.

Intellectual Integrity

Review Questions

1. What is the first piece of armor mentioned by Paul in Ephesians 6:13-15?

2. According to Paul Johnson in *Modern Times*, what is the key attitude of the twentieth century?

3. Explain how the painting of Francis Bacon, "Head VI", expresses the attitude of contemporary man.

4. What is the fundamental difference between modernism and Postmodernism?

5. Explain the meaning of the "line of uncertainty."

6. What are the five stages of the line of uncertainty?

7. Draw the line of uncertainty and put the examples of GREEK philosophers in their proper place.

8. Draw the line of uncertainty and put the examples of MODERN philosophers in their proper place.

9. What is the main epistemological problem of the non-believer?

10. Explain the two basic epistemological options of the non-believer who attempts to know the truth without God, and explain the consequences of each one.

11. Explain the problem of denying the possibility of knowing the truth.

12. Explain the problem of asserting that all views are true.

13. Explain the Christian concept of the truth and draw the corresponding figure.

14. Explain the illustration of G. K. Chesterton regarding the situation of contemporary man.

15. Explain the illustration of Francis Schaeffer about the pages of the book.

16. What important biblical principle about the truth can we learn from Liberation Theology?

17. What does John Calvin say about whether God allows non-Christians to know the truth?

Questions for reflection

1. Have you yourself experienced the stages of the line of uncertainty?

2. Has your concept of the truth changed in any way during this lesson? If so, how?

3. Do you think you are submitted to the Lord in every area of thought?

4. What can you do to help "take every thought captive to Christ"?

CHAPTER 3
THE CHRISTIAN AND HIS RELATION WITH SOCIETY

"They are poor, but make many rich. ... To sum up all in
one word--what the soul is in the body, that are
Christians in the world.."[47]

Epistle of Mathetes to Diognetus,
Second century A.D.

Introduction

When I was in college, students were protesting on
campus against war and speaking against racism. Then I
would go to church on Sunday where our topics of discussion
always seemed far removed from what was really happening
in the "real world." For a while I thought the church was not
going to make much difference in the world. Of course, later I
realized I was wrong.

There have been different views throughout history of
how Christians should relate to society and culture. One
classic book that is very helpful is H. Richard Niebuhr's *Christ
and Culture*.[48] Although it is not a recent book, his book is
often quoted and still serves as a point of reference. Donald
A. Carson says, "Even though Niebuhr's *Christ and Culture* is
more than fifty years old, it is difficult, at least in the English-

---

[47] http://www.earlychristianwritings.com/text/diognetus-roberts.html (Nov. 30,
2006)
[48] Richard H. Niebuhr, *Christ and Culture*, (Harper and Row, New York, 1975).

speaking world, to ignore him. His work, for good and ill, has shaped much of the discussion."[49]

The Five Models of the Relationship between Christianity and Culture

Niebuhr analyzes five historical tendencies with respect to this issue. He actually calls it the issue of "*Christ* and Culture," as Christ is made visible through His body, the Church. The question is, how has Christ's relationship to culture been manifest throughout the history of the Church? He defines "culture" as "the artificial, secondary environment which man superimposes on the natural." He explains that "it comprises languages, habits, ideas, beliefs, customs, social organization, inherited artifacts, technical processes, and values."[50] We could say it displays the "character" and the "personality" of a society.

There are two essential attitudes toward culture in general: either it is basically good or it is basically bad. From these two fundamental attitudes, five positions are derived:[51]

1. Christ Against Culture
2. Christ in Culture
3. Christ Above Culture
4. Christ and Culture in Paradox
5. Christ Transforms Culture

---

[49] D.A. Carson. *Christ and Culture Revisited*. Eerdmans. Kindle edition, Preface and p.10. (Original hardback, 2008, paperback, 2012).
[50] Niebuhr, p. 32.
[51] Actually, he calls models 3, 4 and 5 all "Christ over culture", and then divides them into "synthesis", "dualist" and "conversionist". However, the chapter titles are as I have listed here, and I find those terms more helpful.

1. Christ Against Culture

Defenders of this position emphasize the presence of sin in society and tend to separate themselves from the "world." The world is basically bad. Niebuhr mentions Tertullian (c. 160-220 A.D.) as an example. He encouraged Christians to distance themselves from military service, politics, and the arts, considering it impossible to avoid the corruption present in such activities.[52] Monasticism is another clear example. The conservative Amish who refuse to drive cars, use electricity, or watch television also illustrate this position. Fundamentalism generally falls into this category as well. Niebuhr considers Leon Tolstoy to be a representative of this tendency, since he despised the sciences, philosophy, and the arts, as being useless.[53] Niebuhr calls these people "radicals." [54]

2. Christ in Culture

These people believe that Christ is operating in and through culture, and they minimize the effects of sin. The world is basically good. They think we should cooperate with the current cultural tendencies, instead of fighting against them or running from them. Niebuhr calls them "cultural Christians."[55] One example is the effort in the first few centuries after Jesus to mix oriental religion and Greek philosophy with Christianity, such as in Gnosticism. Liberal Protestant theology of the nineteenth century reflects a similar attitude, because it tends to adapt Christianity to culture and combine it with current secular philosophy. Niebuhr mentions Albrecht Ritschl as the best illustration of

---

[52] Niebuhr, pp. 52-55.
[53] Niebuhr, pp. 62-63.
[54] Niebuhr, p. 75
[55] Niebuhr, p. 106

this view.[56] He says that for Ritschl, loyalty to Jesus leads to active participation in culture.[57] I would say another example is Liberation Theology, which pretends to mix Marxism with Christianity. They see the Marxist movement as God's way of liberating ("saving") the poor and the oppressed.[58]

3. Christ Above Culture

Niebuhr says that representatives of this view supposedly recognize "sin's universality and radical nature", but adds that "express statements are difficult to reconcile."[59] His main objection is that they "do not in fact face up to the radical evil present in all human work."[60] It's not a question of "either-or" but "both-and."[61] Christianity is not opposed to culture, nor does it adapt to it; it is *combined* with it. For them, the world is somewhat good and somewhat bad.

St. Thomas of Aquinas is a good example of this tendency.[62] Niebuhr says, "In his system of thought, he combined without confusing philosophy and theology, state and church, civic and Christian virtues, natural and divine laws, Christ and culture."[63]

Aquinas' use of reason in his theological method illustrates his attitude toward culture. His view and his

---

[56] Niebuhr, pp. 94-101.
[57] Niebuhr, p. 100.
[58] Here are a few representatives: 1. José Míguez Bonino, *Doing Theology in a Revolutionary Situation*, (Fortress Press, Philadelphia, 1975), *Christians and Marxists; The Mutual Challenge to Revolution* (Grand Rapids: Eerdmans, 1976), 2. Gustavo Gutiérrez, *A Theology of Liberation*, (Orbis Books, Maryknoll, New York, 1973), and 3. Juan Luis Segundo, *The Liberation of Theology*, (Orbis Books, Maryknoll, New York, 1976).
[59] Niebuhr, p. 119.
[60] Niebuhr, p. 148.
[61] Niebuhr, p. 120.
[62] Niebuhr, p. 128-140.
[63] Niebuhr, p. 130.

Intellectual Integrity

method have heavily influenced Roman Catholicism even until now. "Faith added on top of reason" would be a good way to summarize it. He leaned heavily on Aristotle, and combined faith and divine revelation with logic, or "added" them to logic. For Aquinas, reason serves us well to lead us to believe in God, for example, but we need faith and special revelation in order to understand aspects like the Trinity.

4. Christ and Culture in Paradox

In this case, while culture is basically evil, we inevitably have to participate in it. We must submit to Christ, but also to culture, even though they are frequently in opposition. Man can't get out of culture, but God sustains him in it. Niebuhr calls this the "dualist" position and says such people are "existential" thinkers.[64] He says, "Hence the dualist joins the radical Christian in pronouncing the whole world of human culture to be godless and sick unto death. But there is this difference between them: the dualist knows that he belongs to that culture and cannot get out of it...."[65] Martin Luther is a key example of this position. Luther taught that man lives in a dilemma, that the Kingdom of God and the Kingdom of the World are clearly distinguishable, but not separable.[66] For him, the hope of a better culture "is not their chief concern," and furthermore "it is impossible for us to live without sinning."[67] Kierkegaard is another representative.

5. Christ Transforms Culture

Representatives of this concept believe that culture is basically evil, but that the grace of God is present too,

---

[64] Niebuhr, pp. 156, 150.
[65] Niebuhr, pp. 156.
[66] Niebuhr, p. 172
[67] Niebuhr, pp. 178-179

Intellectual Integrity

bringing positive transformation. We should not separate ourselves from the world (like position #1), nor go along with it (#2), simply add grace to it (#3), nor reluctantly accept it and submit to it (#4). Instead, we should stay in it and work toward changing it. This change is not just an addition, but a profound transformation. Niebuhr considers John Calvin a representative of this position. He expressed this view, not only in his writings, but in his life, especially in Geneva. He labored for years to convert the city into a model Christian society. Although they made mistakes, they did a lot of good things: they received refugees, took care of the sick and the elderly, transformed the laws of commerce, and even constructed a sewage system. They literally cleaned up the city![68]

Problems with the First Four Models

Probably nobody is fully consistent with any of these positions, and each of them expresses something valid. However, I will defend the fifth position in the rest of this chapter as what I consider the most biblical. First, I will show the problems I see in the other four positions, then I will give some biblical-theological support for the "transformation" view.

1. Christ against Culture

It's true that we live in a fallen world. Scripture tells us to flee from sin and not conform to this world (Romans 12:1-

---

[68] Some reformed theologians such as David VanDrunen and Michael Horton defend a "two kingdom" view similar to Luther and argue that Calvin represents that option. See the following articles: The Resurgence of Two Kingdoms Doctrine: A Survey of the Literature - The Gospel Coalition, A Tale of Two Kingdoms by Michael Horton (ligonier.org), A Review of David VanDrunen's Living in God's Two Kingdoms (ligonier.org)

2). We should respect the strength of character among those who refuse to follow the customs of the world, even when it means being ridiculed sometimes. We can also learn about nurturing our relationship with God through prayer and meditation from those who dedicate themselves to a more monastic lifestyle. We can appreciate our Pentecostal brethren's emphasis on worship and evangelism.

However, Jesus prays, "I do not ask that you take them out of the world, but that you keep them from the evil one" (John 17:15). This first view fails to recognize sufficiently the "common grace" which God has given to every human being, and the merciful care and blessings which He pours out on the undeserving world. It's too negative.

The Bible teaches that each person is the image of God (Genesis 1:26), and that God "makes his sun rise on the evil and on the good, and sends rain on the just and on the unjust" (Matthew 5:45). Jesus indicated that people sometimes do good things, even if they are not really His followers. In such cases, "the one who is not against us is for us" (Mark 9:40).

We should be thankful for all the scientists who developed the vaccines and for the doctors, nurses and others on the front lines of the battle, who risked their lives to save others during the COVID pandemic. I also think we should be more open to information from secular sources. While any source can be wrong and needs to be carefully scrutinized, I observed during the pandemic what I consider an exaggerated lack of trust in the medical authorities and in the news media reporting on the pandemic. The verse that has meant a lot to me is 1 Thessalonians 5:21: "...test everything; hold fast what is good."

Finally, this view does not encourage Christians to change the world. In fact, it leads to just the opposite.

Separating Christians and the accompanying work of the Holy Spirit from the world only makes it worse. Jesus tells us we are the "salt of the earth" and the "light of the world" (Matthew 5.13-14). When this light is removed, darkness prevails.

2. Christ in Culture

This position has the benefit of recognizing God's universal grace among all people. We can learn from them to see more good things in the world (Philippians 4:8), to take more time to understand cultural trends, to appreciate non-Christians and their contributions to society. Again, as mentioned above, in some circumstances, we need to remember that "if they are not against us, they are for us."

Nevertheless, this position doesn't recognize sufficiently the extent and depth of sin in culture. While it is true that God's universal grace works among all people, we can't minimize the effects of the Fall. The attitudes of pride, selfishness, dishonesty and hatred contaminate everything. (Romans 3:12: *All have turned aside; together they have become worthless; no one does good, not even one.*) This is why we are given so many warnings not to be carried along by the current of this world. The Lord wants his people to be *different*. (Romans 12:2: *Do not be conformed to this world….,* 1 John 2:15: *Do not love the world or the things in the world. If anyone loves the world, the love of the Father is not in him.*)

3. Christ above Culture

This view is more complex. It supposedly recognizes sin in the world, but at the same time fails to take its effects sufficiently into account. The Bible doesn't teach us to just add the spiritual aspect to culture or combine the two, but to "renew our minds" (Romans 12:2) and to "take every thought captive to obey Christ" (2 Corinthians 10:5).

To be fair, in practice, many who represent this view are trying to make things better. I have always been impressed with the overwhelming amount of social work done by the Roman Catholic Church, for example. They take very seriously the call to serve others like Jesus did.

However, this view tends to leave much of culture, philosophy, and human reason unredeemed. This can be illustrated by the image of the Virgin of Guadalupe; Mary is standing on the moon, above it, an important symbol in the indigenous religion, showing that she is superior, but she is not transforming it.[69]

4. Christ and Culture in Paradox

It's true that we live in a fallen world, inevitably tangled up with corrupt institutions whether we like it or not, and we will not completely conquer sin until the Lord returns. This perspective is a helpful reminder of the "already – not yet" stage of salvation we are in currently, and of our constant need for God's grace. And Luther did not simply give up in his struggle against sin.

However, it seems too pessimistic about improving the world. It fails to take sufficiently into account the victory of Christ over evil, and it allows us to become passive and discouraged. Scripture is much more hopeful. (Romans

---

[69] Rodolfo Blank, *Teología y Misión en América Latina* (St. Louis: Concordia Publishing, 1996), p. 34.

12:21: *Do not be overcome by evil, but overcome evil with good.* 1 John 5:4: *For everyone who has been born of God overcomes the world.)*

Biblical-Theological Support for Transformation

Keeping in mind that this is somewhat oversimplified and theoretical, it seems to me that the only position that fully recognizes that the world is corrupt, but that we should stay in it to transform it (not just to add something, and not with little hope), is the fifth position. It recognizes that God is operating in the world to accomplish something good, even among unbelievers. It is realistic about evil, but optimistic about God's transforming power. In addition to the texts cited above, there are some fundamental biblical concepts that point to the duty of transforming culture.

1. The Cultural Mandate

As explained in chapter 1, God gave man a special task at creation. Genesis 1:28 has been called the "cultural mandate" (...*Be fruitful and multiply and fill the earth and subdue it....*). God placed Adam in the Garden of Eden to cultivate it, reflecting man's responsibility over the whole earth. But to "subdue the earth" means much more than taking care of the plants and animals. It means being stewards of the whole creation and the development of human society.

2. Man is the image of God.

Not only is transforming culture one of man's basic duties, it is also part of his nature, since he was made in the image of God (Genesis 1:27). He is a reflection of God. This means he has a personality, a sense of humor, a moral

Intellectual Integrity

conscience, a sense of beauty, a complex capacity to communicate, emotions, reason, will, and all that distinguishes man from the animals. It includes his stewardship over all things and his creativity.

Man reveals the image of God in everything he does, in his work, in his play, in relationships, in his thinking, in his art, and in his music. When a person fulfills the cultural mandate, he feels good about himself, since he is expressing the image of God. When he cultivates a garden, fixes a machine, or builds a house, he feels a sense of satisfaction. When he paints a picture, sings a song, or composes a poem, he senses joy. These activities are manifestations of the image of God.

3. Redemption restores all dimensions of life.

All relationships were broken because of the fall: Between man and God, between man and his neighbor, between man and nature, and between man and himself, within his own heart. Conflict replaced the original harmony in every dimension. However, our salvation means that God undoes all the damaging results of sin. In Christ, He restores all of creation and all the consequences of the Fall (Colossians 1:20 and Ephesians 1:10).

Sometimes we emphasize almost exclusively our reconciliation with God (justification) when we talk of redemption. This of course is the most important aspect, and all the other blessings flow from this renewed relationship. But if we minimize the other aspects, our picture of salvation is incomplete. As the Holy Spirit works within our hearts, we do our job better, we become more creative, we love our family more, and we take better care of the world we live in. Notice that the Great Commission includes teaching people to obey God in every aspect of their lives. (Matthew 28:20: ...teaching them to observe all that I have commanded you....)

4. The Kingdom of God is here.

Someone might ask why the Bible doesn't use the term "cultural mandate." I would answer that it teaches the concept without using the terminology. The idea is included in the concept of the "Kingdom of God." That is, the extension of the Kingdom can be seen as fulfilling the "cultural mandate." The Kingdom of God is manifest when God's will is done, and it includes every aspect of life.

When Jesus becomes man, lives a holy life, dies for the sins of His people, and is raised from the dead, He establishes the true Kingdom. He began His public ministry with the message, "Repent, for the kingdom of heaven is at hand" (Matthew 4:17). Jesus confirms His authority as Messiah with the signs of the Kingdom (Matthew 11:11-19 and 12:28) and explains the parables of the Kingdom. He enters Jerusalem as king (John 12) and confesses before Pilate that He is king (John 18:33-37). He is resurrected with all authority in heaven and on earth (Matthew 28:18). He is already reigning and nothing is outside His domain.

There are two parables of the kingdom in Matthew 13 that should encourage us to stay in the world to transform it: the parable of the leavening (13:33) and the parable of the wheat and the weeds (13:24-30 and 13:36-43). While leavening often symbolizes evil in the Bible, in this case it symbolizes the extension of the kingdom. It affects the whole loaf of bread, or in this case three measures of flour, enough to make bread for 100 people![70] Christians are meant to be dispersed throughout the world, making everything better. And the lesson we learn from the parable of the good plants

---

[70] France, R. T. (1994). Matthew. In D. A. Carson, R. T. France, J. A. Motyer, & G. J. Wenham (Eds.), *New Bible commentary: 21st century edition* (4th ed., p. 922). Inter-Varsity Press.

and the weeds is that during this age we are not meant to be totally separated from evil people and non-believers. Rather, we remain mixed in among them until the "end of the age."

Review Questions

1. Name the five models of the relation between Christ and culture, according to Richard Niebuhr, explain each one briefly, and give an example for each one.

2. Explain the problems with the first four models, according to the author.

3. Name and explain the biblical-theological points that support the fifth position, according to the author.

Questions for reflection

1. What is your opinion regarding the author's arguments against the first four models of the relation between Christ and culture and in defense of the fifth position?

2. Which of the five positions best represents your life up to this point? What do you think you should change?

CHAPTER 4
NON-CHRISTIAN WORLDVIEWS

During an early period of my life, I was afraid to read philosophy and non-Christian literature, because I thought I might lose my faith. I remember once when I started reading *Nausea* by Jean Paul Sartre; it really did make me feel sick! I had to put it down, and only years later could I finally pick it up and read it. However, after understanding more about other worldviews, I have seen that non-Christian philosophies don't have a solid foundation and there is really nothing to fear. In this chapter, we'll briefly survey some of the most common worldviews and compare them to Christianity. We will focus on the basic aspects of their belief systems.

Common Non-Christian Worldviews

In *The Universe Next Door*,[71] James Sire explains some of the most common worldviews. In this chapter, we'll summarize these perspectives, drawing especially on Sire's analysis, but we will also add other worldviews that Sire does not include. Then we'll examine some fundamental problems with the non-Christian views and offer an apologetic strategy to defend our faith.

Sire defines a "worldview" as a "commitment, a fundamental orientation of the heart, that may be expressed as a story or in a set of presuppositions (assumptions...) that we hold ... about the basic constitution of reality, and that

---

[71] James Sire, *The Universe Next Door; a Basic Worldview Catalogue* (Downers Grove, Illinois: InterVarsity Press, 1997).

provides the foundation on which we live and move and have our being."[72]

He says there are seven fundamental questions that, when answered, reveal a person's life focus:

a. What is prime reality – the really real?
b. What is the nature of external reality, that is, the world around us?
c. What is a human being?
d. What happens to a person at death?
e. Why is it possible to know anything at all?
f. How do we know what is right and wrong?
g. What is the meaning of human history?

He explains eight worldviews:

1) Christian theism
2) Deism
3) Naturalism
4) Nihilism
5) Existentialism
6) Eastern pantheistic monism
7) New Age
8) Postmodernism

1. Christian Theism

Christian theism holds that there is a personal God who is transcendent but immanent, omniscient, sovereign, and good. God created the universe out of nothing to function according to laws of cause and effect, but in an open system. This means that the universe is not chaotic, but neither is it

---

[72] Sire, p. 20.

programmed in a fatalistic way in which man has no freedom. Man has been created in the image of God with personality, intelligence, a moral sense, sociability, and creativity. Man can know the world and God because God created him with that capacity. Man was created good, but because of the Fall, the image of God was disfigured. In Jesus Christ, God redeemed man and began the process of restoring His people. Death is the doorway to another life, either a life with God and His people, or a life separated from God. Ethics are based on the character of God. History is linear, a sequence of events that leads to the fulfillment of God's purposes.

2. Deism

For deists, God created everything but then left it running like a great machine. God is transcendent, but not personal. The cosmos that God created is determined and closed, without God's intervention, and without the possibility of miracles. Man is part of the great machine of the universe. The world is in its normal state, not fallen or abnormal. We can know the universe and decide what God is like through scientific study of the universe. Ethics is also revealed in the universe; what is, is correct. History is linear, and the course of history was already determined at creation. Deism was very influential in France and England at the beginning of the eighteenth century, but it was superseded by naturalism.

3. Naturalism

According to naturalism, matter has existed from eternity, and that is all that exists. God does not exist. The cosmos works according to the laws of cause and effect, and it is closed. Man is nothing more than a complex part of material reality. Personality is an interaction of chemical and physical properties. Death is the extinction of personality and individuality. History is a linear stream of events, without purpose. Ethics is derived from human experience, and basically consists of doing what is convenient, in what produces harmony. Atheistic evolutionism is an example of naturalism.

4. Nihilism

Nihilism is more a sentiment than a philosophy, accepting the fact that nothing has meaning. In fact, it is a negation of philosophy, of the possibility of knowledge, and of all value. It is expressed in the sculpture of Marcel Duchamp, "Fountain," which is nothing more than a common urinal, or in the drama of Samuel Beckett, "Breathing," in which there are 35 seconds of sound: first a cry, then breathing in, then breathing out, and finally one more cry. That's life. Nihilism is the result of accepting the practical consequences of atheistic naturalism. *If everything is matter, then nothing matters,* not even my own philosophy. Nietzsche is the precursor of this sentiment, who declared that God was "dead".[73]

5. Existentialism

There are two forms of existentialism: atheistic and theistic. Atheistic existentialism holds that the cosmos only contains matter, but somehow a human being has a consciousness. That is, he is aware of himself and he thinks. The external world seems absurd to him, but the authentic man rebels against the absurd and creates his own values and his own meaning as an individual. Man can't continue

---

[73] Sire, 94-116.

living with the conviction that nothing makes sense. Therefore, existentialism arose as an effort to overcome Nihilism, proposing that man himself must determine his own meaning. Sartre and Camus represent this approach. Theistic existentialism is really quite different. This view accepts many aspects of theism, but distrusts human reason. Faith is subjective and individual, and truth is a paradox. Søren Kierkegaard represents this second school of existentialism.[74]

6. Eastern pantheistic monism

According to pantheistic monism, there is only one kind of being, and an impersonal deity is in everything. This is the most popular approach in the East. According to Sire, eastern religions go even further than existentialism in their distrust of reason; they totally renounce the fight for the truth. Furthermore, they tend to give up the fight to change the world; they prefer to simply exist. The Zen branch of Buddhism says: "Atman is Brahman", the soul of every human being is the soul of the cosmos. The whole cosmos is good, and there are no real contradictions. Man is not aware of his unity with the cosmos and must wake up to that reality. They try to reach a state of mind in which they feel no distinctions between good and evil, truth and falsehood, reality and illusion.

7. The New Age

The *New Age* is a western version of oriental religions, but with emphasis on the individual, which for them is the primary reality. The cosmos manifests itself in two ways, the visible universe, accessible by means of the normal

---

[74] Sire, 117-143.

conscience, and the invisible universe, accessible through altered states of consciousness (for example, with drugs). Man must realize that he is God. "Know that you are God; know that you are the universe," says Shirley MacLaine.[75] In contrast with pantheism, the New Age accepts the animistic concept of the existence of many spiritual beings.

8. Postmodernism

Whereas "modernism" began with philosophers like Descartes who trusted primarily in reason and science, "Postmodernism" no longer trusts reason, and has no definite worldview. Postmodernists no longer care about what reality is like (ontology) or about how you can know the truth (epistemology). Man is what he decides he is. Ethics is determined by society; we decide what is correct.[76]

Other Worldviews

We could add some other worldviews to Sire's excellent review:

a) Animism

The term "animism" comes from "anima" ("soul"). They believe that everything, including animals, plants, rocks, and all objects, have spiritual life. Some people estimate that 40% of the world's population today is animist. Frequently this religion includes witchcraft, magic, superstition, and rituals. Normally they believe in one creator god who is over many small gods. Nevertheless, man cannot relate to the creator, but only to the smaller gods of health, weather, and all that affects his daily life. For some, animism is another form of

---

[75] Sire, p. 155.
[76] Sire, 214-243.

pantheism, because everything that exists contains the universal soul of God. [77] [78]

b) Religions that share some biblical revelation

There are other religions that are practiced by a large number of people, such as Islam, Judaism, Mormonism, and the Jehovah's Witnesses. These religions also use portions of biblical revelation, and therefore also share some aspects of our worldview. However, their teachings are quite different in important areas. It's beyond our scope to compare these religions here, but the key differences between them and orthodox Christianity lie in the content of the revelation they have accepted or added, in their view of nature of Jesus Christ and the Trinity, and in the means of salvation. Only orthodox Christianity preaches a God who is a Trinity and a gospel of grace, in which salvation is by faith.[79]

Problems with Non-Christian Worldviews

All non-Christian views produce contradictions, either with the world we live in, with the nature of man and our God-given instincts, or logically within their own system of thought. But Christianity is completely coherent.

First, all of creation reveals the true God. An atheistic or impersonal worldview can't explain the signs that the universe was made by an intelligent designer. How did everything come to be so magnificently formed? Think of the human body, plants and animals, the fine-tuned physical laws, or how the planets remain in their orbits. According to

---

[77] http://religion-cults.com/Ancient/Animism/Animism.htm

[78] J.N.D. Anderson, The World's Religions (Grand Rapids: Eerdmans, 1968), pp. 9-24.

[79] See the section "World Religions and Competing Worldviews" in Dockery, David S; Wax, Trevin. Christian Worldview Handbook (p. 138). B&H Publishing Group. Kindle Edition.

Romans 1:18-20, God has revealed Himself in the creation in a way that mankind can even capture something of His "invisible attributes," his "eternal power and divine nature." Paul appeals to this in Athens, when he talks to the philosophers about the "unknown god" (Acts 17:16-34). Psalm 19 says, "The heavens declare the glory of God; the sky above proclaims his handiwork." To deny a personal God while living in a personal world is like a prodigal son denying that he has a father. To deny the existence of the true God inevitably comes into conflict with God's revelation in the creation and with a person's sense of His existence. At one time, people thought the earth was the center of the universe. But when scientists began to look at the evidence, things just didn't fit. In the same way, a worldview that leaves out the true God just doesn't fit. God is our center.

Romans 1:19-20

For what can be known about God is plain to them, because God has shown it to them. For his invisible attributes, namely, his eternal power and divine nature, have been clearly perceived, ever since the creation of the world, in the things that have been made. So they are without excuse.

Secondly, some views contradict *the nature of man and his instincts.* Man is the image of God, and all the special characteristics that distinguish him from animals (reason, morality, creativity, and emotions, for example) point to the personal Creator. An impersonal atheistic worldview can't explain the personal aspects of man. Where did his emotions come from, such as love and happiness and anger? C. S. Lewis testifies that an important factor in his conversion was discovering joy and realizing that it had to come from outside

Intellectual Integrity

himself, which pointed him to God.[80] Paul tells us that God has engraved on man's heart something of His law, a sense of right and wrong, a conscience. Any worldview that denies that there is such a thing as right and wrong, or any ethical system that contradicts the moral principles that the Creator has written on man's heart, inevitably comes into conflict with those God-given instincts.

Romans 2:15
They show that the work of the law is written on their hearts, while their conscience also bears witness, and their conflicting thoughts accuse or even excuse them.

Thirdly, consider how some non-Christian worldviews contradict themselves logically within their own system of thought; *they self-destruct*. Worldviews that believe in some kind of impersonal unity in the universe, without a transcendent God outside of that world, face an inevitable logical dilemma. The problem is that man would also be trapped inside this impersonal thing, whether it be something organic, mechanical or immaterial. He could not be outside of it. Consequently, he would be impersonal too, and he could not have the characteristics that make us human, such as our capacity to reason and make decisions, to be creative, and to feel emotions. This means he couldn't really trust or defend his own thoughts and reasoning.

---

[80] C. S. Lewis, *Surprised by Joy* (Orland, FL: Harcourt Brace and Company, 1955).

For example, if deism is true, or some form of naturalism, like atheistic evolution, the universe is determined impersonally like a huge organism or like a huge machine. This would mean that man's thoughts are nothing more than a chemical reaction or a mechanical movement like the ticking of a clock. As Cabanis put it crudely, "The brain secretes thoughts in the same way that the liver secretes bile."[81] Therefore, how can we believe that our thoughts are correct? Why would we think they even mean anything? In fact, the very theory that we are proposing is itself just a chemical reaction. This is like sawing off the branch we're sitting on!

Darwin himself wrote in a letter:

The horrendous doubt will always arise whether the convictions of the human mind, which has evolved from the mind of inferior animals, really has value or is

---

[81] Cabanis, quoted in Sire, p. 98 (without indicating the original source or the complete name). He may be quoting Pierre Jean George Cabanis, a French philosopher.

to be trusted. Should one trust in the convictions of the mind of a monkey, if convictions exist in such a mind? [82]

As we saw in chapter two, the ancient Greek philosophers understood this problem, and it led them into skepticism. Heraclitus sustained that the universe was in constant movement like a river. Everything flows. "You can't step twice into the same river."[83] Then Gorgias decided that all knowledge and communication was impossible.[84]

Why? Because I can't believe that the universe is a great flowing river, and at the same time also pretend that I am standing on the riverbank, outside the river, observing the flow in an independent and objective way. I must also be a part of the river too. And if I am only part of the river, how can I pretend to give my opinion about the nature of the river? Cratylus was consistent with this scheme when he decided to stop talking![85]

C. S. Lewis explains the contradiction of Naturalism:

If all that exists is Nature, the great mindless interlocking event, if our own deepest convictions are merely the bye-products of an irrational process, then clearly there is not the slightest ground for supposing that our sense of fitness and our consequent faith in uniformity tell us anything about a reality external to ourselves. Our convictions are simply a fact about us —

---

[82] Quoted in Sire, p. 83. Sire attributes the quote to a letter written to W. Graham (July 3, 1881), which in turn is quoted in *The Autobiography of Charles Darwin and Selected Letters* (New York: Dover, 1892, new edition, 1958).

[83] Humberto Giannini, *Esbozo para una historia de la filosofía* (Santiago, Chile, 1981), p. 17.

[84] Humberto Giannini, p. 25.

[85] Humberto Giannini, p. 34.

like the colour of our hair. If Naturalism is true we have no reason to trust our conviction that Nature is uniform. [86]

He also argues:

The Naturalist cannot condemn other people's thoughts because they have irrational causes and continue to believe his own which have (if Naturalism is true) equally irrational causes. [87]

Lewis quotes the argument of J. B. S. Haldane:

If my mental processes are determined wholly by the motions of atoms in my brain, I have no reason to suppose that my beliefs are true...and hence I have no reason for supposing my brain to be composed of atoms. [88]

Finally, as mentioned before, the views that question the very possibility of certain knowledge have a more obvious problem. If I can't be sure of anything, how can I be sure that I can't be sure of anything? It's a self-contradiction, like saying, "everything I say is a lie!"

Existentialists recognize these problems, but they also know that man can't live with this complete uncertainty. Therefore, without being able to defend it rationally, they make a blind leap of faith. The problem with the existentialist view is that anything can be true. If everyone invents his own values, and decides for himself what is true, then anything is

---

[86] C. S. Lewis, *Miracles* (New York: MacMillan, 1968), p. 108.
[87] C. S. Lewis, *Miracles*, p. 22.
[88] *Possible Worlds*, quoted by Lewis in *Miracles*, p. 22.

Intellectual Integrity

true. But if anything is true, then the concept of truth loses its meaning.

The Christian view is coherent and sustainable.

Only the Christian view fits the world we live in and allows for true knowledge and freedom, without contradicting itself. We don't have to accept a worldview that leads to contradictions or a blind leap of faith. The Christian view is not monist, but affirms that there are two kinds of reality: God and His creation. Man is not simply part of one huge organism, machine, or evolving spiritual being. He is a creature of God, made in His image, with freedom of thought, with the use of reason, and with emotions. The world is very personal, because the personal Creator made it to reflect His own attributes. And man does not have to look within himself to find the truth, nor does he have to know everything to be sure of something; God, who is the source of all truth, reveals His truth to man.

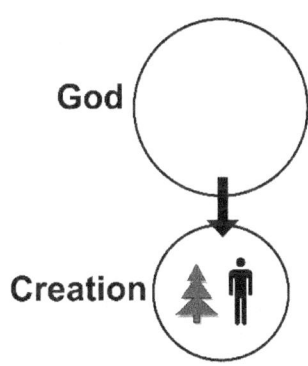

As we defend our faith, we can ask the other people why they believe what they believe. When they explain why, saying for example that they accept scientific evidence, or that their view is logical, we can ask how they can be sure the scientific evidence is valid or why they trust their logic. We can keep pushing them to their final answer. This is not a game; we should do this with much love and respect. Otherwise, we will lose the opportunity to explain the gospel. But if we continue asking until there are no more questions, where does the non-believer end up? What is his "final answer"? He will have to back up to something beyond which he has nothing more to say in defense of his view.

Expressed in one way or another, that final answer for the non-believer will essentially be that he believes he himself is the judge of what is true and of what is right or wrong. As in the Garden of Eden, man still pretends to be the judge of things, in spite of the fact that his Creator is right there.

This of course eliminates all certainty with him, because to be sure of anything, he really needs to know everything. This leads to inconsistency within himself, because he instinctively knows that he doesn't know everything, that he is not God, and that he can't simply decide for himself what the truth is.

The Christian alternative is to accept God as judge and as the source of truth. When you keep pushing a Christian to his "final answer," it should be that "God says so." It's true because God says so. How do I know God says so? Because He says He says so! I can't back up any further than what God Himself says in His Word. I can't put anything above Him. If I appeal to another authority superior to the Word of God in the Scriptures, I have just shattered the foundation of my own worldview and contradicted my philosophy of life.

Furthermore, only Christianity proclaims a personal loving God who is a Trinity and a gospel of grace in which salvation is by faith alone. Only Christianity has the true answer for the needs of the world: the need for forgiveness, for salvation and for radical change. All other worldviews leave people uncertain, guilty and hopeless.

A Suggested Apologetic Approach: "DEFEND"

I would like to suggest several aspects to keep in mind as we dialogue with non-Christians. These may change in their order, and it might not always be necessary to include them all. It depends on how the conversation goes. Furthermore, these points may be covered over a period of time in a series of conversations.

1. Demonstrate interest.

Ask questions to get acquainted. Find out about his or her family, interests, and religious background. Most people enjoy talking about themselves and their family. Be genuinely interested in the person, not just in a hurry to "convert" him. They can always tell if you are sincere. People are fascinating! Remember that they are the image of God, and worthy of our love and respect.

2. Explain your faith.

Share your testimony. Try to find a natural transition to share about your own life, your family, and your religious experience. Most people will begin asking you questions as the conversation continues. Explain how you understand the gospel.

3. Furnish answers to his questions.

Hopefully at this point, the person will become curious and ask questions. He or she may express doubts, or even criticism of the Christian faith. It's important to accept these comments gracefully and not take them personally. Do your best to provide reasonable answers.[89]

4. Expose his basic presuppositions.

Now it's your turn to ask questions. I recommend asking the person *why* he believes what he believes. Then ask again why he believes the second principle. Continue this pathway until he comes to the end, until he can't give any other reason. For example, he might believe in evolution. Then when you ask why, he gives scientific evidence. Then you can ask why he trusts scientific evidence. Eventually, he will somehow reveal his basic starting point. This will inevitably be some form of trusting himself as the final judge of the truth. If possible, try to bring to person to recognize this. This process will very likely make the person very uncomfortable. You are stripping away his cover, forcing him to expose his deepest convictions. Furthermore, these convictions probably have remained practically unconscious until now, and it may be extremely unnerving to face them. Try to be gentle, but without backing down.

5. Navigate through the inconsistencies of the non-Christian view.

Again, you must be sure that you don't show pride or disdain. If we don't show love and humility, it doesn't really matter whether our arguments are solid or not; they won't listen to us. But still, we need to gently show him where the non-Christian position is inconsistent. You are like a medical doctor who has to discover the patient's sickness. You won't help the patient by denying his sickness, but keep in mind

---

[89] For suggested answers to some of the most difficult questions, see the author's book, *The Certainty of the Faith; Apologetics in an Uncertain World* (Phillipsburg, N.J.: P&R Publishing, 2007).

Intellectual Integrity

that nobody likes to hear bad news. You are like John Nash's wife, pointing out the fact that the imaginary child in his pretend world has not grown up. Something is seriously wrong with his scheme. Basically, the non-Christian has been hanging on to beliefs that are self-contradictory, and he has developed a worldview that he cannot live with consistently. For example, if he believes in evolution because he believes in science, and he believes in science because he trusts his senses and logic, you can point out the fact that if evolution were true, his own thoughts would be a part of that impersonal process, and therefore they lose their meaning. If evolution is true, then his thoughts are no more significant than the tick tock of a clock or a grape growing on a vine. These pieces don't fit.

6. Direct the person to Christ.

It would be terribly cruel to expose the contradictions of the non-believer, then leave him with no solution and no hope. He needs to know that Jesus has died for us and risen again. His unbelief is not neutral, but it's a rejection of his creator. Remind him of the story of Adam and Eve, and gently show him that he is also questioning his creator in an illegitimate way. But the good news is that there is forgiveness and restoration. He can be reconciled with God by trusting in Jesus and what He has done on the cross. He can begin a new life with the important things in proper perspective. His planet can be returned to its proper place in the solar system. He can be born again and submit his heart and mind to God. His basic problem is spiritual, not intellectual. And the solution is spiritual, a personal relationship with Christ.

1 Corinthians 2:1-5

And I, when I came to you, brothers, did not come proclaiming to you the testimony of God with lofty speech or wisdom. For I decided to know nothing among you except Jesus Christ and him crucified. And I was with you in weakness and in fear and much trembling, and my speech and my message were not in plausible words of wisdom, but in demonstration of the Spirit and of power, that your faith might not rest in the wisdom of men but in the power of God.

You can remember these points by using the acrostic "DEFEND":

Demonstrate interest.

Explain your faith.

Furnish answers.

Expose his presuppositions.

Navigate through his inconsistencies.

Direct him to Christ.

Actually, the most difficult aspects of our apologetic task have already been taken care of by the Holy Spirit. First, according to the Scriptures, we don't really need to convince anybody that God exists, because deep down, they already know it. God has revealed Himself to every human being, through creation and in his own heart. The problem is that they suppress this inward truth and try to hide it (Romans 1:18-25, Acts 17). Secondly, man has a moral sense, a conscience, and therefore also a sense of guilt. Even though the values may be distorted, there is at least a general sense of right and wrong.

Intellectual Integrity

Romans 2:14-15

For when Gentiles, who do not have the law, by nature do what the law requires, they are a law to themselves, even though they do not have the law. They show that the work of the law is written on their hearts, while their conscience also bears witness, and their conflicting thoughts accuse or even excuse them.

Even tribal groups far removed from civilization manifest a sense of guilt and a need to somehow make a sacrifice to cover their sin. One group may send out a dog on a raft to die for them. Others may cut off the head of a chicken. Some even sacrifice their own children. One of the most astounding things I have ever seen was a frozen indigenous child found in the Andes Mountains. I saw him in a museum in Chile. The experts believe he is hundreds of years old. He was dressed and seated in a way that shows he had been sacrificed to the gods.

Since God has given man an innate sense of His own existence, and an innate sense of right and wrong, we don't need to hammer away at those points. We can gently help a person take away his protective mask and uncover them. We can also humbly help him see the problems and contradictions in his own worldview. Then we focus on showing him Christ and the gospel.

Review Questions

1. Explain the main postulates of each of the worldviews analyzed by James Sire.

2. Explain the beliefs of animism.

3. Explain the most important differences between orthodox Christianity and religions that share portions of biblical

revelation, such as Islam, Judaism, Mormonism and the Jehovah's Witnesses.

4. Explain how impersonal atheistic worldviews contradict the world we live in.

5. Explain how impersonal atheistic worldviews contradict the nature of man and his God-given instincts.

6. Explain how worldviews that consider the universe as an impersonal unit, without a personal God transcending it, contradict themselves.

7. According to Romans 1 and 2, what are the two important things that God has revealed to all mankind?

8. Explain why the Christian view is the only coherent and sustainable view.

9. Explain the apologetic method called "DEFEND".

Questions for Reflection

1. Would you like to know more about other worldviews not included in this chapter? Which ones?

2. Do you think some aspects of other worldviews might be attractive to some people? Which aspects? Why?

3. Do you see other problems or contradictions in the non-Christian worldviews? Explain.

4. Do you have other suggestions about apologetic methods?

5. Do you agree with the author in his analysis of the problems in non-Christian worldviews? Why?

6. Do you agree with the author in his analysis of why the Christian view is coherent and sustainable? Why?

Exercise

Ask two people to volunteer to practice a dialogue. One person will be a Christian and the other person will take on the role of a non-believer. The Christian should practice the "DEFEND" steps, discovering the approach of the non-believer, showing him his inconsistencies, and presenting the gospel to him.

In the second half of this book, we'll be analyzing politics, economics, science and art. These chapters give an introductory look at some general principles that can hopefully be applied to a variety of situations. They are meant to be *examples* of how to work toward developing a Christian perspective on the subjects. I don't pretend to be an expert in any of these areas, but I want to give you some things to think about, especially some Bible passages related to the subjects. Hopefully the reader will be encouraged to continue studying these topics and come to his or her own conclusions regarding the issues.

CHAPTER 5
TOWARD A CHRISTIAN VIEW OF POLITICS

When I first arrived in Chile as a missionary in 1978, the country was still living under the military regime of Augusto Pinochet (From 1973 until 1990). Naturally, I was curious to hear what the Chileans thought about the situation. But when I began to ask questions, people didn't want to talk about politics, because the topic was too controversial. To this day, Chileans are still extremely sensitive about their views of the political situation at that time.

Politics is even more divisive in other countries. A missionary recently told me that in some churches in the country where he serves, people from different political parties sit on different sides of the isle during worship services.

In the United States, I have observed that some churches and some denominations are so evidently aligned with a political party that people from another party don't feel comfortable among them. People have left their church because their pastor didn't openly express support for the political cause they embraced.

These are extremes: either keep quiet or argue, either agree or split. It seems like we should be able to talk about politics without fighting or dividing, and we don't have to agree on everything. In this chapter, we'll examine issues such as the task of the government, its relation with the kingdom of God and the Church, and how Christians should try to have a positive influence in it. We'll look at some basic lessons we can learn from the Bible and from history.

The Task of the Civil Government

Abraham Kuyper, who was a pastor, theologian, and prime minister of Holland, distinguished between an "organic" development and a "mechanical" development of social institutions. On the one hand, the institutions that have developed in an "organic" way are necessary and "natural." They would have developed even without the existence of sin. On the other hand, the institutions that have developed in a "mechanical" way are those that are necessary only because of sin. These are like stakes that a gardener places alongside a new small tree so that it will grow straight.[90]

Kuyper argues that even without sin and the results of the Fall, society would have become organized organically, but as one large family in patriarchal form. However, for Kuyper, the State[91] as we know it now, with police, courts, and armies, includes aspects that are only necessary because of sin. In other words, they developed in "mechanical" form.[92]

I think the distinction between "mechanical" and "organic" development is helpful. We can only speculate about how people would have organized society without sin,

---

[90] Abraham Kuyper, *Lectures on Calvinism*, "Calvinism and Politics," and "Politics," talks at Princeton, 1898. <http://www.kuyper.org/main/publish/books_essays/article_17.shtm >, (July 1, 2010).

[91] Terminology can be confusing in the study of politics. Sometimes the term "State" includes the people and territory that are governed, as well as the institution that governs them. Kuyper seems to be using the term that way in this context. The term "civil government" normally refers more specifically the institution that governs the State. Sometimes the two terms are used synonymously. Our main concern in this chapter is the civil government.

[92] See "Abraham Kuyper and Herman Bavinck on Church and State," Jessica Joustra, The Gospel Coalition, Canadian Edition, Feb. 7, 2023. <https://ca.thegospelcoalition.org/article/abraham-kuyper-and-herman-bavinck-on-church-and-state/> (Feb. 21, 2026)

but we can assume they would have obeyed the mandate to "be fruitful and multiply," to "fill the earth" and to "subdue it." Furthermore, the image of God in people would have led them to keep things orderly. As the human race grew, life would have become more complicated, requiring more organization and supervision.

To give some examples, they probably would have established guidelines for the exchange of products. People would have learned to cooperate in the care of their sheep and the cultivation of wheat, possibly in the education of their children. They would have organized many things in a similar way that they have done now after the Fall, but without the damaging effects of sin. *This would have been a positive organic development of society.*

Unfortunately the Fall did occur, and that changes things. Now we also need laws to protect people from each other and to combat the effects of sin. We need police and judges to make sure the laws are enforced and that justice is maintained. *This is the negative mechanical development of society.*

This perspective suggests that there are also two aspects of the *task* of the civil government, negative and positive. This is exactly what we find in the New Testament. Paul wrote:

Romans 13:3-6
For rulers are not a terror to good conduct, but to bad. Would you have no fear of the one who is in authority? Then do what is good, and you will receive his approval, for he is God's servant for your good. But if you do wrong, be afraid, for he does not bear the sword in vain. For he is the servant of God, an avenger who carries out God's wrath on the wrongdoer. Therefore one must be in subjection, not only to

avoid God's wrath but also for the sake of conscience. For because of this you also pay taxes, for the authorities are ministers of God, attending to this very thing.

Peter writes something similar. He says the authorities of human institutions, including the emperor and his governors, are sent by God "to punish those who do evil and to praise those who do good" (1 Peter 2:13-14).

In 1 Timothy, Paul urges the readers in Ephesus to pray for government rulers so that they might lead a "peaceful and quiet life."

1 Timothy 2:1-2
First of all, then, I urge that supplications, prayers, intercessions, and thanksgivings be made for all people, for kings and all who are in high positions, that we may lead a peaceful and quiet life, godly and dignified in every way.

Notice the negative and positive aspects:
1) Rulers are a "terror" for wrongdoers and "bear the sword" to punish them.
2) Rulers are God's servants "for your good," and they should help you live a "peaceful and quiet life."

In order to restrain evil, they need to establish laws and enforce them. For example, the government establishes laws against stealing, then when someone robs another person, the authorities should punish him. The authorities also set speed limits and install stoplights to make the roads safe. When people disobey these guidelines and make things dangerous for others, they deserve to be punished.

Note that there is an exception to obeying the authorities. When they command you to do something against God's will, you should obey God first. Peter himself was one of the apostles that refused to stop preaching the gospel (Acts 4:19-20, 5:29).

Providing a "peaceful and quiet" environment points to the positive task of *protecting freedom and maintaining peace and order.* In 1 Timothy, Paul's exhortation was made in the context of persecution, and he was urging them to pray for freedom to worship in peace and to live according to their Christian convictions. The government has the duty to protect religious freedom, even for minority groups. But the phrase also suggests *maintaining peace and order* in general.

To be "servants for your good" clearly means protecting people from the harm of evildoers in the context of Romans 13, but I think it also includes the task of *maintaining peace and order.* The government needs to provide services that help society develop and function properly. Some things can't be managed without the government, such as establishing borders, making sure people have water and electricity, or building bridges and highways, for example.

In summary, the main tasks of the civil government are to *restrain evil, protect freedom, and maintain peace and order.*

Notice that this description of the task of civil government doesn't imply that the government has the overarching task to manage every aspect of society or take care of every need. There are other institutions such as the Church and the family that also play an important role in caring for people.

In fact, the education of children is actually seen as the parents' responsibility in the Scriptures (Deuteronomy 6:6-7, Ephesians 6:4, Proverbs 22:6). This doesn't mean that it's necessarily wrong for the government to organize public schools or for Christian parents to send their children to public schools, but rather that they should stay informed about their children's education and discuss important topics with them. They should help them form a Christian worldview, just as we are proposing in this book. It also means that the government should allow families to do home-schooling and churches to organize private Christian schools.

The government should play the role of a *referee*. Normally he lets the athletes play freely (protect freedom), but he has to make sure they play by the rules (maintain peace and order) and sanction them when they don't (restrain evil). In general, I would propose that the government should not interfere in the normal activities of people and institutions, except when some injustice or disorder exists between them. For example, the government shouldn't tell whether you should buy a mobile phone or where you should buy one. However, if you steal one from a store, you should be held accountable. Your "freedom" has become a lack of freedom for the store owner. As someone said, "My right to swing my arm ends where your nose begins."[93] Normally, the government should allow businesses to operate freely, but the moment the owners begin to abuse their workers or do something harmful or unjust, the government should step in to correct the situation.

---

[93] Several people have made similar statements, and it is not clear who first said it. <quoteinvestigator.com> "Your Liberty To Swing Your Fist Ends Just Where My Nose Begins" (Sept. 9, 2021)

Politics and the People of God; A Lesson from the Old Testament

Israel had the privilege of being God's special People during the period of the Old Testament with whom God made His covenant. They began as a *family*, a patriarchal tribe (Genesis). Later they became organized as a nation, with laws to restrain the effects of sin (Exodus) and with a structure of appointed leaders (Numbers). Here they became what we call a "theocracy," in which God named the leaders and guided them directly. There was one official religion, the worship of Yahweh. Moses was a prophet, liberator, and ruler, but he served God as His direct representative. Upon entering the Promised Land, God raised up judges to rule over Israel (Judges 2:16).

The next stage was a monarchy. Previously, while under the leadership of Moses, God had told them they would ask for a king one day and that their request would be granted.

Deuteronomy 17:14-15

When you come to the land that the LORD your God is giving you, and you possess it and dwell in it and then say, "I will set a king over me, like all the nations that are around me," you may indeed set a king over you whom the LORD your God will choose.

Several centuries later, as was prophesied, they ask for a king "like all the nations" (1 Samuel 8:5). Here we read something curious: God grants their request, but He expresses discontent with the idea. God tells Samuel,

1 Samuel 8:7

...Obey the voice of the people in all that they say to you, for they have not rejected you, but they have rejected me from being king over them.

God also warns them through Samuel of the consequences of having such a king. He will send their sons out as soldiers, running before his chariots. He will put them to work making weapons and cultivating crops. He will "appoint for himself" military commanders and send others to plow "his" ground. He will call their daughters to be perfumers, cooks, and bakers. He will demand a tenth of their crops and their flocks, and they will be his "slaves" (verses 10-17). They will not be happy with this arrangement.

1 Samuel 8:18

And in that day you will cry out because of your king, whom you have chosen for yourselves, but the LORD *will not answer you in that day.* (vs. 18)

But even after this warning, the people still ask for a king to judge over them and lead them into battle, "like all the nations" (v. 20). God tells Samuel to grant their request, even though it was wrong of them. Surely the motive to be "like all the nations" was offensive to Him. It was like "serving other gods" (v. 8). Nevertheless, He lets them have a king.

Why? We know that sometimes God grants our inappropriate requests in order to teach us a lesson. In this case, it would make them aware that it's not such a good idea to be like the other nations. They were supposed to be different!

This is also an example of something we see all through Scripture: God allows things that seem bad at the time, then turns them into something good. The best example is the crucifixion of Jesus; it was the worst sin ever committed, but it accomplished our salvation. In the case of letting Israel have a king "like the other nations," it was wrong of them to ask for this, but God turned it into something good: He prepared His people to live under secular rulers, to function as the salt of the earth among all nations.

From the beginning, God's plan always was to disperse His people throughout the world to bring positive change. God promised Abraham that all the families of the world would be blessed in him (Genesis 12:2-3). To accomplish this, His people would need to be weaned away from a theocracy. Eventually, God's people would not only have a king like the "other nations"; they would actually be *living* in these "other nations."

The period of the monarchy is not completely bad, especially under David and Solomon. However, the nation becomes corrupt, with many evil kings and constant violence, then suffers a tragic division.

Finally, they were defeated by foreign nations and taken into exile. They lost their identity as a monarchy, having no king of their own. Some later returned to Jerusalem and rebuilt the walls and the temple, but it was not like before. They suffered under the dominion of several different empires, including the Romans who were ruling at the time of Christ.

When their Messiah came, the Jews rejected Him. Pilate asked them, "Shall I crucify your King?", and the chief priests answered, "We have no king but Caesar" (John 19:15). Then Pilate turned Jesus over to be crucified. Paul explains that the Jews "stumbled" over Jesus (Romans 9:30-33). Now there is "neither Jew nor Greek" (Galatians 3:28); all believers are united in Christ (Ephesians 2:11-22). Jesus died to ransom people "from every tribe and language and people and nation" (Revelation 5:9).

What does this brief historical sketch teach us? It clearly points to the need for salvation and to the need for Jesus as the perfect King. But what does it teach us about politics?

First, it teaches us that God graciously uses civil governments to accomplish His purposes, but they will inevitably be imperfect, corrupted by sin. In fact, the ideal government will never be established in this fallen world; we will have to wait until Christ returns. Meanwhile, like Abraham, we live "as in a foreign land," "looking forward to the city that has foundations, whose designer and builder is God." We desire a "better country, a heavenly one" (Hebrews 11:8-16).

Secondly, God's special covenant People is no longer a political nation or an ethnic group. God de-centralized His people and left them without a king They only had prophets, priests, and elders. But this actually extended their realm of influence. Synagogues were established in different countries throughout the Mediterranean area, which eventually became platforms for preaching the Christian gospel message. Then Jesus gave His followers the Great Commission to make disciples of "all nations" (Matthew 28:19).

GOD'S SPECIAL COVENANT PEOPLE

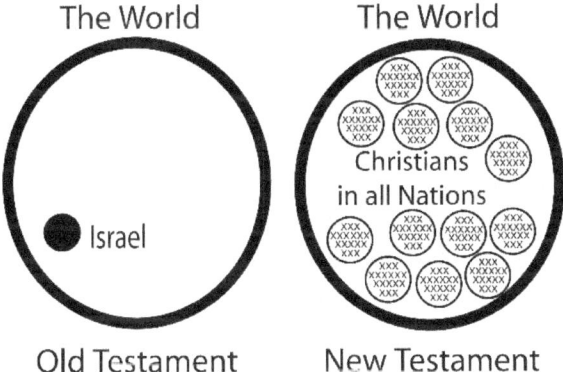

This has important practical implications today. It means that *no country and no ethnic group can claim the privilege of being God's special chosen People now.* However, it also means that *God's people, as Christians, are spread throughout the world in ALL political nations.*

The people of God are not any one nation,
but they are *in* all nations.

Politics and the Kingdom of God; A Lesson from the New Testament

Just as the *People of God* can no longer be identified with a political nation, neither can the *kingdom of God* be identified with a political movement or a political party.

People often misunderstood the nature of Jesus' kingdom. Herod the Great tried to kill Him as a baby, because he was afraid He might eventually replace him as king over Judea (Matthew 2:1-12). Satan tempted Jesus by offering Him "all the kingdoms of the world" if He would fall down and worship him, but Jesus rebuked him (Luke 4:4-8). When Pilate asked Him if He was king of the Jews, Jesus answered, "My kingdom is not of this world," then added, "if my kingdom were of this world, my servants would have been fighting, that I might not be delivered over to the Jews" (John 18:33-36).

Even the disciples misunderstood this. In Acts 1:6-8, they ask Him if He is going to restore the kingdom to Israel. They apparently expected Him to initiate a movement to end the oppression of the Romans and restore the nation of Israel to something like the monarchy under David. They were probably confused with His answer at first. Maybe they even thought He misunderstood them.

Acts 1:6-8
So when they had come together, they asked him, "Lord, will you at this time restore the kingdom to Israel?" He said to them, "It is not for you to know times or seasons that the Father has fixed by his own authority. But you will receive power when the Holy Spirit has come upon you, and you will be my witnesses in Jerusalem and in all Judea and Samaria, and to the end of the earth."

Is He saying that they shouldn't be concerned with the coming of the kingdom? Or that the only important thing now is evangelism? Of course not. It may have been hard for the disciples to comprehend at first, but He understood the question perfectly and He was actually explaining *how the kingdom of God would be established.*

It's not by force nor with weapons, not by temporal means nor politics, but by testifying about Jesus. The Holy Spirit was going to come with more power than ever, and He would take them to every corner of the world with the

Intellectual Integrity

message. That's the way His kingdom will be established. The only way to bring true change to society is through a spiritual change in peoples' hearts.

But it doesn't end with conversion; that's just the beginning. The epicenter of change is the heart, but the effects ripple through the family, the church, and all of society, including politics, social media, business, education, science, medical care, art, literature, ...everything. As God reigns in the heart, every aspect of a person's way of thinking and living is transformed. Jesus taught the disciples to pray, "Your kingdom come, your will be done, on earth as it is in heaven" (Matthew 6:10). When God's will is done, His kingdom comes.

For example, suppose that a very selfish man is the owner of a shoe factory, in which he doesn't pay his workers a fair wage or treat them with respect. The only thing he wants to do is make more money. The workers can protest and plead with him to be fair, but he won't care. However, if he becomes a Christian, his attitude will change, then he will pay them better and treat them better. This is the coming of the kingdom!

A secretary glorifies God, not only by being nice to her colleagues or by sharing the Good News with them (without denying the importance of these things), but also while carrying out her regular tasks, however tedious and insignificant they may seem at the moment. Why? Because she is manifesting the image of God and because her work benefits society. It's a way to fulfill the cultural mandate and extend the kingdom of God.

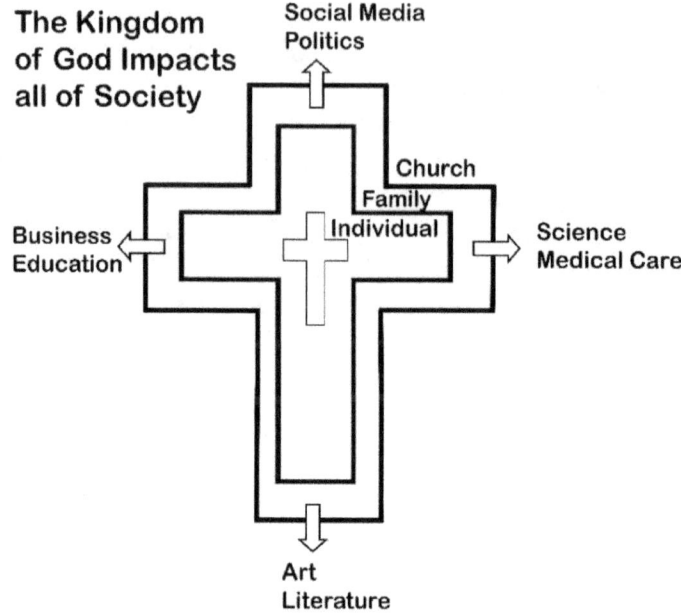

The kingdom of God cannot be identified with any political movement. God's special instrument for establishing His kingdom is not politics. Instead, it's the power of the Holy Spirit transforming people through the preaching of the gospel, who in turn transform the world around them.

However, this doesn't mean politics are insignificant, or that the civil government is no concern of ours. *The kingdom of God permeates the world of politics, just as it transforms all areas of society.*

> The Kingdom of God is not *of* this world,
> but it *transforms* the whole world.

How Should Christians Relate to Their Civil Government? A Lesson from a Coin

How should Christians relate to their civil government? I would argue that in general, we should apply the same principle that we defended regarding culture and society in general. That is, instead of staying away or going along with the secular influence, we should work to transform our government to make it better. *Politics don't change people, but people change politics.*

When the Pharisees and Herodians asked Jesus if it was lawful to pay taxes to Caesar (Matthew 22:15-22), He asked them to show Him a coin and answered them with another question: "Whose likeness and inscription is this?" When they answered that it was Caesar's image on the coin, He wisely replied, "Therefore render to Caesar the things that are Caesar's and to God the things that are God's."

They were trying to trap Him. On the one hand, the Herodians were supporters of Rome and would consider it illegal to refuse to pay taxes. On the other hand, the Pharisees hated Rome and would consider it offensive and immoral to support Caesar. They thought they had Him cornered, but they didn't.

How did Jesus outwit them? Notice that He doesn't say that they should refuse to pay taxes to such a pagan government or that they should overthrow the Roman Empire. But neither does He allow them to think that they can recognize Caesar as their highest authority. Notice that neither the Herodians nor the Pharisees were able to criticize His answer; they were amazed and went away.

I don't think Jesus means they should keep these two aspects of their lives totally separate, as if to say, "follow the government rules for *secular* matters and follow God's rules for *spiritual* matters." He's not suggesting that there are two separate kingdoms.

So what does Jesus mean? He is putting things in their proper place. If the coin has the image of Caesar, it belongs to him. But Caesar has the image of God on his person, and therefore Caesar belongs to God! Jesus reminds them of the fact that God is sovereign over all things, including the Roman Empire.

Donald Carson explains that this passage doesn't warrant an "absolute dichotomy between God and Caesar, or between church and state, or between Christ and culture." He adds that "if we give back to God what has *his* image on it, we must all give ourselves to him. ...We may be obligated to pay taxes to Caesar, but we owe everything, our very being, to God."[94]

Jesus is admitting that it's legitimate to pay taxes to Caesar. Paul confirmed this in Romans 13. But He is teaching something more profound: you can live under a civil government and fulfill many civil duties of this kind, without betraying your commitment to God. This points again to the concept of being "in" the world to transform it, but not "of" the world. It also fits the plan for Christians to be dispersed and live under different kinds of civil governments in different countries.

But to do this requires being faithful to God above any worldly ruler. If the civil authorities require us to do something against God's will, we are obligated to refuse. When the authorities forbid the disciples to preach in the name of Jesus, they disobeyed in order to put God first (Acts 4:19, 5:29).

---

[94] Carson, *Christ and Culture Revisited*, p. 57.

The Relation Between "Church and State"; A Lesson from History

The question of how the Church should relate to the civil government has been debated throughout history (often expressed in terms of the relation between "Church and State.") Does the government have authority over the Church? Does the Church have authority over the government? Should there be a "wall of separation" between them?

During the first few centuries after Christ, Christians in the Roman Empire were persecuted for their religious beliefs and practices, or tolerated at best. They were often punished because they refused to worship the roman gods and the emperor. Under Constantine, Christianity was legalized (the Edict of Milan, 313) and became protected by the emperor. He had the authority to organize the Council of Nicaea in 325 to resolve theological issues. In 380, Christianity became the official religion of the Roman Empire (The Edict of Thessalonica).

During the following centuries, the Church became a powerful institution that had a very close relationship with the civil government. Normally the government had the upper hand, but sometimes the Church did. For example, the Church seemed to have authority over the state when they initiated the Crusades (1095) and called on the civil leaders to carry out the battles. However, the inquisition in Spain (beginning in 1478) was established by the monarchy to preserve their Catholic beliefs and punish Jews, Muslims, and later also Protestants. In this case, the civil magistrates had authority over religious affairs.

At the time of the Reformation, the close relationship between Church and State still continued, and the Church was abusing its power. But instead of recognizing the deeper need to remove the religious aspect of the role of civil government, the reformers just tried to change the official religion of countries, which produced wars and persecution. The Anabaptists went to the other extreme, insisting that Christians should separate themselves entirely from the affairs of civil governments.

John Calvin was beginning to discern a solution to this problem, but he wasn't totally consistent. He proposed that the civil magistrates govern the matters of "outward morality," and that the Church govern the affairs of "inner man."[95] However, when Calvin speaks of the task of the civil government, he includes the prevention of blasphemy and religious offenses. This contradicts his distinction, because these are matters of the "inner man." Furthermore, he agreed with the city council in Geneva when they sentenced Michael Servetus to death for holding a heretical view of the Trinity.[96]

A century later, his followers in England drafted *The Westminster Confession of Faith*. They proposed that the civil government should not "interfere in matters of faith" or establish a preferred denomination, but protect the Church and guarantee its freedom.

> Civil magistrates may not assume to themselves the administration of the Word and sacraments; or the power of the keys of the kingdom of heaven; yet he has authority, and it is his duty to take order that unity and peace be preserved in the Church, ...

---

[95] *Institutes*, IV, XX, 1.

[96] "Why did John Calvin have Michael Servetus burned at the stake for heresy?" Got Questions. <https://www.gotquestions.org/Calvin-Michael-Servetus.html> (March 14, 2026).

Yet, as nursing fathers, it is the duty of civil magistrates to protect the Church of our common Lord, without giving the preference to any denomination of Christians above the rest, in such a manner that all ecclesiastical persons whatever shall enjoy the full, free, and unquestioned liberty of discharging every part of their sacred functions, without violence or danger. [97]

However, similar to Calvin, they still didn't limit the authority of the government sufficiently, in my opinion. According to the early versions of the *Confession*, the civil magistrate even had authority to supervise ecclesiastical councils, suppress religious error and prevent abuse in worship. He should guarantee...

...that the truth of God be kept pure and entire, that all blasphemies and heresies be suppressed, all corruptions and abuses in worship and discipline prevented or reformed, and all the ordinances of God duly settled, administrated, and observed. For the better effecting whereof, he has power to call synods, to be present at them and to provide that whatsoever is transacted in them be according to the mind of God.[98]

After the Reformation, the Protestant Church began to make the limits clearer. In fact, later versions of the *Westminster Confession*, as early as 1788, took out the section quoted above regarding suppressing heresies and

---

[97] *Westminster Confession of Faith,* Chapter 23, section 3. Version of 1646. <http://www.spurgeon.org/~phil/creeds/wcf.htm#chap23>, (July 1, 2010).
[98] *Westminster Confession of Faith*, Ch. 23, section 3. Version of 1646. <https://www.blueletterbible.org/study/ccc/westminster/Of_The_Civil_Magistrate.cfm> (Feb. 27, 2026)

abuses in worship, as well as the right to call synods.[99] They made it very clear that the government should not "in the least interfere in matters of faith." Read the same section quoted above, but in a version adopted in 1788:

> Civil magistrates may not assume to themselves the administration of the Word and sacraments; or the power of the keys of the kingdom of heaven; *or, in the least, interfere in matters of faith.* Yet, as nursing fathers, it is the duty of civil magistrates to protect the church of our common Lord, without giving the preference to any denomination of Christians above the rest in such a manner, that all ecclesiastical persons whatever shall enjoy the full, free, and unquestioned liberty of discharging, every part of their sacred functions, without violence or danger. And, as Jesus Christ hath appointed a regular government and discipline in his church, no law of any commonwealth, should interfere with, let, or hinder, the due exercise thereof, among the voluntary members of any denomination of Christians, according to their own profession and belief. It is the duty of civil magistrates to protect the person and good name of all their people, in such an effectual manner as that no person be suffered, either upon pretense of religion or of infidelity, to offer any indignity, violence, abuse, or injury to any other person whatsoever: and to take order, that all religious and ecclesiastical assemblies be held without molestation or disturbance.[100]

---

[99] Lee Irons, "The 1788 Revision of the Westminster Standards," <http://www.upper-register.com/papers/1788_revision.pdf> (July 1, 2010).
[100] The 1788 American Revision of the Westminster Standards, p. 10. *Westminster Confession of Faith*, chapter 23, section 3. < Microsoft Word - 1788_revision.doc (upper-register.com) >, (Oct. 18, 2023).

When the Americas were colonized, many countries began with an official state religion, mostly Roman Catholic, but almost all eventually changed their constitutions to eliminate the policy of an official religion.[101] In the United States, there existed a variety of denominations. Thomas Jefferson wrote about the "wall of separation" between religion and the government. The First Amendment of the constitution says the following:

> Congress shall make no law respecting an establishment of religion, or prohibiting the free exercise thereof; or abridging the freedom of speech, or of the press; or the right of the people peaceably to assemble, and to petition the Government for a redress of grievances.[102]

I think this brief historical sketch demonstrates that it's not a good idea for either the Church to have authority over the State or for the State to have authority over the Church. However, I don't think the image of a "wall of separation" is the best metaphor to explain the proper relationship between them. Such a phrase sounds like neither institution should have any influence in the other, as if the wall were impenetrable. I prefer to speak of "boundary lines" instead of "walls," and of mutual respect instead of complete "separation." Abraham Kuyper used the term "sphere sovereignty" for human institutions. In my opinion, the most

---

[101] "State Religion" in *Wikipedia*: < http://en.wikipedia.org/wiki/State_religion > (July 1, 2010).
[102] "U.S. Constitution Online," <http://www.usconstitution.net/const.html#Am1> (July 1, 2010).

Intellectual Integrity   113

important point is to protect the Church from the interference of the State in matters of faith and worship.

How to Apply the OT Laws Today

There's an important issue to address as we consider how to influence for better laws: how should we apply the laws of the Old Testament today? I often witness confusion regarding this matter. I cringe when a pastor is interviewed on TV and doesn't know what to say when the reporter asks him about the Old Testament punishments for certain kinds of immoral behavior.

Some theologians, such as the "theonomists," believe that we should apply the laws of the Old Testament now in basically the same way as in the ancient times, and that we should try to influence our governments to establish laws to fulfill that purpose.[103] On the other extreme are those who believe that the laws of the Old Testament have no application for us today; they were only for the Jews at that time.[104]

John Calvin proposed a more balanced solution. He made a distinction between three aspects of the Old Testament law: the ceremonial aspect, the civil aspect, and the moral aspect.

Since Jesus made the last sacrifice (Hebrews 9:24-28), we do not have to keep the *ceremonial* aspect of the law. That is, we no longer make sacrifices, and we no longer observe the rituals and ceremonies related to the temple.

In a similar way, since the People of God is no longer one political nation (Israel), but rather believers from all

---

[103] See, for example, Greg Bahnsen, *Theonomy in Christian Ethics* (Nutley, N.J.: Craig Press, 1979), p.73.
[104] See for example Lewis Sperry Chafer, *Systematic Theology*, 8 vols. (Dallas: Dallas Seminary Press, 1948) 4:166, 208-210.

nations, we no longer need to keep the *civil* aspect of the law as they did before Christ. This aspect was related especially to things like the stipulated punishments and the management of properties. For example, we no longer are required to punish adultery or homosexual relations by death (Leviticus 20:10,13). There were laws related to properties that we no longer need to observe, such as the Year of Jubilee (Leviticus 25), in which property was to return to its original owner every fifty years, Hebrew prisoners were to be set free, and debts were to be cancelled.

However, the *moral* aspect of the law should still be observed as in the Old Testament period. These universal ethical principles reflect the character of God and are for all people in all times. Although we don't need to observe the details of the civil laws, they still contain lessons for us regarding *general principles of justice*. For example, stealing is still a sin and being selfish with our material possessions is still a sin. Furthermore, while we don't need to observe the details of the ceremonial laws either, they still teach us *spiritual truths*. For example, the sacrifices point to the sacrifice of Jesus on the cross. In other words, we do not apply the civil and ceremonial laws in the same way that they were supposed to back then, but we can find helpful teachings in them.[105] The *Westminster Confession of Faith* also makes this three-way distinction. (See chapter 19.)

---

[105] John Calvin, *Institutes of the Christian Religion,* (IV,20,15). See also *Commentaries on the Four Last Books of Moses Arranged in the Form of a Harmony,* trans. Charles William Bingham, 4 volumes (Edinburgh: The Calvin Translation Society, 1843) 1:498-502.

Three Aspects of the O.T. Law

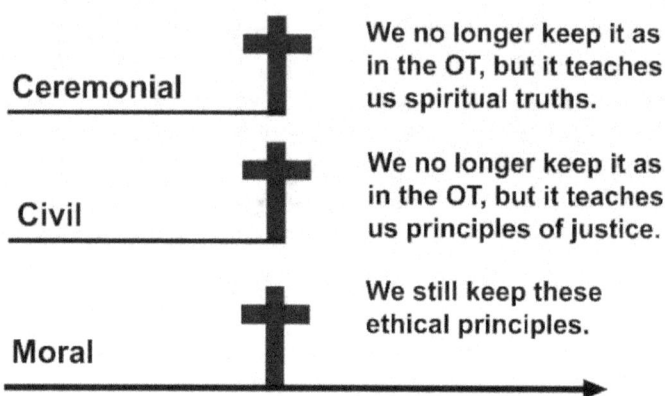

Ceremonial — We no longer keep it as in the OT, but it teaches us spiritual truths.

Civil — We no longer keep it as in the OT, but it teaches us principles of justice.

Moral — We still keep these ethical principles.

This changes the way we try to influence in the laws of the civil government. We shouldn't ask the government to apply the civil aspects or the ceremonial aspects of the law in the way required in the Old Testament.

What Form of Government is Best?

There are different ways to categorize forms of government, and it can be confusing, because some of them overlap. The following are important terms to help classify governments: [106]

Monarchy: Throughout history, including Bible history, most governments have been monarchies. This means either

---

[106] See https://www.merriam-webster.com/dictionary, https://examples.yourdictionary.com/, Wikipedia.org, https://thebestschools.org/magazine/common-forms-of-government-study-starters/, https://www.scholastic.com/teachers/articles/teaching-content/government/

a king or queen inherits the right to rule by being next in line of succession within the royal family. In an absolute monarchy, the ruler has power over everything, but in many monarchies, the power is limited by a constitution or by other branches of the government.

Republic: In a republic, the power to rule rests in the people, who elect representatives to govern, following the guidelines of a constitution, and they do not have a king or queen.

Democracy: This also refers to a system of government in which the power rests in the people. There are basically two kinds: a) In a "representative democracy," the people elect representatives to make decisions for them. While some make a distinction, for our purposes in this book, we will consider "representative democracy" synonymous with a "republic." Over half the nations of the world today fit this description. b) In a "direct democracy," people vote directly on all issues, instead of electing representatives to make decisions for them.

Dictatorship: In this form of government, one person or a small group of people has absolute power. In contrast with a typical monarchy today, the power to rule in a dictatorship is obtained by force and is exercised by force, as in a military dictatorship for example.

Totalitarianism: This term describes the extent of power exercised by the ruler or rulers. It means they intend to control every aspect of society, including the media and the economy, leaving little personal freedom, and using repressive means to accomplish it. This could take the form of a dictatorship, but it could also take the form of a government ruled by just one party.

Which is best?

Knowing the power of sin and selfishness, I think a government that includes a constitution, a system of checks and balances, and a wider sharing of the power to make decisions, like a republic or representative democracy, is normally better. Furthermore, after considering the task of the civil government, it seems wise to keep their power limited and guarantee a healthy amount of personal freedom. Totalitarianism is dangerous. However, we should also be careful not to assume we know exactly how these principles should be applied in contexts and cultures that we don't know or understand.

Other Practical Suggestions

After becoming Christians, part of our spiritual growth includes our responsibility as citizens of our country. We can work toward improving our government without confusing politics with the kingdom of God. While we can't expect politics to transform people, we should definitely expect transformed people to make a positive impact on their government.

But how? Here are some suggestions:

a) One important way we can have a positive influence in our government is by informing ourselves and voting responsibly. I recommend examining the candidates' policies and their history. I also think their character is just as important. It's their personal integrity that will determine how they make decisions and how they act as politicians. A candidate might make promises that we support, but if he is dishonest, he won't keep them.

b) There may also be occasions when it's appropriate to write to an elected official or participate in a *peaceful* protest.

c) Some Christians may even be called to hold public office, like Abraham Kuyper in Holland and many other Christians throughout the world.

d) We should "renew our minds" and teach biblical guidelines for ethical and social issues.

e) The Church also has a prophetic role in denouncing injustice and defending freedom and morality. However, when churches, pastors or leaders speak publicly or in representation of the People of God, we should be certain that we can defend what we say from Scripture, just like when we preach a sermon from the pulpit. *The Westminster Confession of Faith* recommends that church councils are not to "intermeddle" In civil affairs except in "extraordinary" cases.

> Synods and councils are to handle, or conclude nothing, but that which is ecclesiastical: and are not to intermeddle with civil affairs which concern the commonwealth, unless by way of humble petition in cases extraordinary; or, by way of advice, for satisfaction of conscience, if they be thereunto required by the civil magistrate.[107]

f) I think it's a mistake when churches and church leaders publicly identify themselves with particular candidates or political parties. After spending time in many countries, I can testify that this can cause the Church to lose its credibility with a large part of the population, as well as its prophetic voice. Furthermore, you can never be sure how that candidate will actually behave during his time in office. We should keep ourselves above the divisive politics of this world, free to denounce sin and injustice on the part of any

---

[107] Chapter 31, section 4. in the current version used by the *Presbyterian Church in America*. < WCFScripureProofs2022.pdf (pcaac.org) >, (Oct. 18, 2023).

politician or political party, and welcome to give spiritual counsel to any politician. We are citizens of a better kingdom. As Carl Trueman says, "The gospel cannot and must not be identified with partisan political posturing."[108]

g) If we as Christians want to help make our government better, we should encourage our politicians to make laws and policies that are aligned with God's Word. However, these laws should deal with justice and order between people and institutions, not personal matters or private religious matters where nobody is harmed or treated unjustly.

h) I would agree with Calvin's statement that the civil government should only supervise *outward* morality. (As mentioned previously, he wasn't consistent with this.) This means that not every sin needs to have a civil law against it. For example, the government shouldn't punish someone for having sinful thoughts like envy, lust, or anger. Our thoughts can be sinful, but they shouldn't be punished as a crime. However, murder definitely should be punished. The government shouldn't punish people for believing in another religion instead of Christianity. In general, we shouldn't let the government decide what we believe or how we worship. However, if a member of another religion kills a Christian because they believe their religion requires it, they should be punished for it.

In the United States, for example, we could try to influence for improving laws regarding topics such as abortion, just economic guidelines (see the next chapter for more on the subject of economics), euthanasia, rights for women, racism, the care of the sick, and war.

i) It's important to respect freedom of religion, even for other religions. I think we should try to influence for more

---

[108] Carl R. Trueman, *Republocrat; Confessions of a Liberal Conservative* (Philipsburg, NJ: P&R Publishing, 2010), p. xxv.

Christian values and more Christian morality, but that doesn't mean we should impose our faith on others.

Os Guinness, in *The Case for Civility*, argues that it is more important now than ever that Christians insist on our freedom of expression and freedom of religion, *and that we also grant this same freedom to others.* He considers that this is one of the most important issues of our day, and he is concerned that some Christian groups in the United States are confused regarding this topic. In the first place, we should treat others as we would want them to treat us, and this includes allowing freedom of conviction and religious practice. In the second place, if we do not protect this freedom for all people, it might be the Christians who lose our rights next time.[109]

Review Questions

1. What is the distinction that Kuyper makes between a "mechanical" development and an "organic" development of social institutions?
2. What are the key biblical passages for understanding the task of the civil government?
3. According to the author, what are the tasks of the civil government? What analogy does he use?
4. What does the history of Israel teach us about the identity of the People of God?
5. What does the New Testament teach us about how the kingdom of God is established?
6. What did Jesus teach from a coin about the relationship of Christians with the civil government?
7. Describe briefly how the Church and State were related in the first few centuries, then from the time of Constantine

---

[109] Os Guinness, *The Case for Civility*.

until the reformation, then during the reformation, and finally after the reformation.

8. According to Calvin, what is the difference between the task of the civil government and the task of the Church?

9. What did the original version of *The Westminster Confession of Faith* say about the duty of the State in relation to the Church?

10. How did later versions of the *The Westminster Confession of Faith* modify the statements in the original version regarding the authority of the civil magistrate?

11. According to the author, how should the civil government relate to the Church?

12. Describe the three aspects of the OT law and explain how they should be applied today.

13. Briefly describe the following terms: monarchy, republic, democracy (representative and direct), dictatorship, and totalitarianism.

14. What are the author's general observations about the characteristics of a good form of government?

15. What are the practical suggestions the author gives for how Christians should try to influence in the civil government?

Questions for reflection

1. What is your opinion about the task of the civil government?

2. What is your opinion regarding the relationship between Church and State?

3. What do you think the government's role should be in areas such as education and medical care?

4. When, if ever, should the government become involved in restricting television, the Internet, and other means of communication? Give an example.

5. At what point do business practices become a matter for government intervention? Mention an example.
6. What form of government do you think is the best? Why?
7. Has your perspective on politics changed after studying this chapter? How?
8. Is the subject of politics very controversial in your church? What are the attitudes you face when dealing with this topic?

Economics is another potentially divisive subject. The Bible has been used and abused to defend a wide variety of economic viewpoints. We need to have a humble attitude, willing to listen and dialogue. Our initial thoughts on what the Bible has to say about economics might be regarding the Old Testament laws for Israel, some Proverbs about being honest and responsible, the prophets' exhortations about helping the poor, Jesus' teachings that we should not be anxious regarding material things, and that we should help the needy. We might also think of how the early church shared all things (Acts 2:44-45 and 4:32-35) and how Paul exhorts us to give voluntarily and cheerfully (2 Corinthians 8:1-15).

In this brief introduction, we'll explain two basic economic philosophies, capitalism and socialism, as well as related subjects like inflation and why Latin America is poorer than the United States. We will analyze some biblical passages and give some tentative suggestions. This is meant as an introduction to initiate a respectful conversation on this complex subject.

Capitalism

In capitalism, the means of production and the distribution of goods are privately owned and operated. The key value for this economic system is *freedom*. While capitalist principles were practiced in many places previously, Adam Smith (from Scotland) is considered the philosophical proponent of the concept. In 1776, he published *The Wealth of Nations*, in which he proposed the idea of an "invisible hand" that guides the economy according to personal interest and benefit. He also observed the "law of supply and demand": when the demand is greater, prices increase, and when the supply is greater, or when there is more competition, the prices drop. He believed that if everyone seeks their own good, everyone will eventually benefit. Competition and free enterprise are healthy for society.

> "It is not from the benevolence of the butcher, the brewer, or the baker, that we can expect our dinner, but from their regard to their own interest."[110]

Capitalism gave energy to the industrial revolution in England, along with the steam engine. Production and consumption increased 1,600% in England during the 19th century. Fabric production shops opened in Belgium and France, and steel factories opened in Germany. In the United States, they built canals and railways. The sad side of the industrial revolution was the abuse of workers, including children who worked long hours in the British factories. These are the problems that Karl Marx observed and that moved him to propose another economic system.

There are a variety of different expressions of capitalism. Some countries allow more government control than others. Even capitalist governments control certain aspects of the economy, such as the construction of highways, the management of the post office, or other important services and utilities. Many restrict monopolies, regulate other aspects of commerce, and ensure proper health care and retirement benefits. While the terminology

---

[110] Adam Smith, *An Inquiry into the Nature and Causes of the Wealth of Nations,* Harvard Classics, vol. 10 (New York: P. F. Collier and Son, 1909), 20.

seems contradictory, some even call the current Chinese economy "state capitalism."[111]

Capitalists argue that their system produces an incentive to work harder, and that it has improved the economy and lifestyle in many countries, which is difficult to refute. For example, Paul Romer points to Hong Kong, a Chinese city governed by the British during the twentieth century. With low taxes, less restrictions, and laws that protected private property, the residents of Hong Kong became ten times wealthier than the rest of the country. This experiment was so successful that China decided to copy the model in other regions. According to Romer, the result has been a great improvement in the whole economy of China, helping around 100 million Chinese overcome extreme poverty (defined by an income of $1 a day or less).[112]

Critics of capitalism suggest that it has produced an unjust inequality, where "the rich get richer and the poor get poorer." For example, some like to point out that, in the United States, the richest 1 percent of the population holds more than one-third of the wealth, while the bottom 50% holds only 2 percent of the total wealth.[113]

Socialism

In socialist systems, many aspects of the means of production, the distribution of goods, and beneficial services, are controlled by the government. The key value for socialism is *equality*. They emphasize cooperation and social

---

[111] Sebastian Mallaby, "The Politically Incorrect Guide to Ending Poverty" *Atlantic* 306 (July/August, 2010): 102.

[112] Mallaby, "The Politically Incorrect Guide to Ending Poverty": 96-98.

[113] < Trends in the Distribution of Family Wealth, 1989 to 2019 | Congressional Budget Office (cbo.gov) > (published September, 2022, vieOct. 20, 2023)

service, and they try to avoid excessive differences between the rich and the poor.

In the 18th and 19th centuries, several authors had encouraged social experiments, in which participants shared all their possessions, divided the work equally among themselves, and shared all their means of production and objects of consumption. This is sometimes called "utopian socialism."[114]

However, Karl Marx (1818-1883) later became the most famous proponent of socialism. He studied history according to empirical laws and concluded that the economic structure is the fundamental basis of society. He emphasized class struggle as the cause of change.[115] He observed the abuses of the industrial revolution in England, and along with Friedrich Engels, wrote the *Communist Manifesto*. They assert in the *Manifesto*, "The history of all hitherto existing society is the history of class struggles."[116] He believed that religion was the "opium of the people," and that to be truly happy, it was necessary to "abolish religion", because it was an "illusory happiness." The true salvation of man will be the formation of a new just society.[117] For Marx, the revolution was inevitable. The proletariat (lower classes) will eventually

---

[114] Encyclopaedia Britannica,
<http://www.britannica.com/EBchecked/topic/620790/-utopian-socialism> (June 1, 2010). Three authors from France, Francois Babeuf (1760-1797), Henri de Saint Simon (1760–1825), and Charles Fourier (1772-1837), as well as Robert Owen of Wales (1771-1858), defended socialism, as a reaction to the problems they observed in the beginning of the industrial revolution.

[115] Arthur F. McGovern, *Marxism, an American Perspective* (Maryknoll, New York: Orbis Books, 1980), pp. 11-36.

[116] *Manifesto of the Communist Party*, chapter 1, in *The Marx and Engels Reader*, ed. Robert C. Tucker (New York: W.W. Norton and Company, 1978), 473.

[117] Karl Marx, *Critique of Hegel's Philosophy of Right*, from *Cambridge Texts in the History of Political Thought, Marx, Early Political Writings*, ed. Joseph O'Malley (Cambridge: Cambridge University Press, 1994), 57-58. See also McGovern, *Marxism*, p. 20.

Intellectual Integrity

rebel against the bourgeoisie (the ruling classes). Marx was less clear about exactly how to establish socialism after the workers took power. He spoke of the "dictatorship of the proletariat" as a transitional step toward the ultimate disappearance of the State, but did not explain details.[118]

Followers of Marx developed greatly differing strategies. In Germany, Engels supported reform without revolution. The Social-Democrat party was formed, which sought political power within the system, without promoting a violent revolution. On the other hand, in Russia, Lenin believed that a "vanguard" party of intellectual revolutionaries should stir up the poor to defend themselves, and that a violent revolution was necessary to achieve socialism. Later, Stalin established a cruel totalitarian rule; he sent millions to Siberia and executed many leaders.[119] Some estimate that about 20 million died in labor camps and by forced collectivization, famine and executions under his regime.[120]

It's important to distinguish between extreme forms of socialism, in which the state controls everything, and moderate forms, in which services such as health and education are controlled by the state, but not everything. We should also note that some countries tend to go back and forth between more capitalistic economies and more socialist economies, depending on the political party that is dominating at the time. The term "communism" has come to be associated with the extreme forms of socialism combined with a totalitarian government ruled by one party.

---

[118] McGovern, *Marxism*, p. 37.

[119] McGovern, *Marxism*, pp. 51-64.

[120] "Major Soviet Paper Says 20 Million Died As Victims of Stalin," New York Times, Feb. 4, 1989. <https://www.nytimes.com/1989/02/04/world/major-soviet-paper-says-20-million-died-as-victims-of-stalin.html> (4/12/2021)

Europe

European countries have been difficult to label during the past century. One author expressed the following analysis in 1951:

> To many people in the United States, European socialists seem dangerously close to communism, and a menace to the American way of life. American officials abroad, however, have reason to know better. They have found European socialist leaders among the most valuable supporters of American policies in the cold war against communism. ... In fact, socialists nowadays are chiefly interested in social welfare and a degree of economic planning.[121]

In other words, they have adopted more moderate forms of what some would call "socialism," which have little to do with Marxism or Leninism. The leaders come to power through democratic processes, and basically, they have economic systems that seek to eliminate drastic differences between the rich and the poor. The key is in charging higher taxes and providing more services, especially education and medical care. In Denmark, for example, individual income taxes vary between 38% and 59%. In Norway and Holland, they can be as high as 49% or 52%, respectively.[122] [123]

A later article published by the *University of Cambridge Press* divides Europe into three categories:

---

[121] Socialism in Europe - The Atlantic, Feb., 1951.
[122] "The Complete Worldwide Tax and Finance Site":< http://www.worldwide-tax.com> (June 1, 2010).
[123] Sarah Pruitt, "How are Socialism and Communism Different?" [https://www.history.com/news/socialism-communism-differences]

Roughly speaking then, Europe is divided into three zones according to the degree of power of democratic socialism: Eastern Europe—bordered on the West by a line running from Trieste to Lübeck—where the democratic Socialist parties have been absorbed by the Communist parties; Northwestern Europe—Great Britain and the Scandinavian countries (Norway, Sweden, Denmark)—under predominant Socialist influence; and the rest of Continental Europe where the Socialists are a more or less powerful opposition group.[124]

More recently, the influence of right-wing parties has been growing in a number of European countries.

Suggestions

Defenders of socialism insist that their system seeks greater equality and that their priorities are nobler, giving more attention to medical care, education, food, and general basic services. Critics say that the results have not been positive, not even producing much help for the poor. Even moderate forms of socialism often produce a lack of incentive and longer complicated processes to obtain services.

I would say that if the system is not working, everyone suffers. But neither is it fair to have a system that works well, when the benefits are mainly for a small minority. Winston Churchill said, "The inherent vice of capitalism is the unequal sharing of blessings; the inherent virtue of socialism is the

---

[124] Democratic Socialism in Europe | World Politics | Cambridge Core, extract of article published July 18, 2011.

equal sharing of miseries."[125] We need a strong economy that protects personal freedom and encourages initiative, but one that also guarantees compassion and justice.

Why is Latin America Comparatively Poor?

This question is important as a case study for economics. It will help us understand several important issues. Furthermore, it has become a test to see what economic convictions and presuppositions people have.

a. An Answer of Liberation Theology

Liberation Theology shows their Marxist orientation by answering that the reason Latin America is poorer than the United States and Europe is basically injustice and oppression on the part of the capitalist countries. According to José Míguez Bonino, for example, capitalism favors the powerful and elevates economic production above human development.[126] The poorer countries live in dependence on the wealthy countries, who manipulate the economy for their own benefit. Bonino claims that, since colonization, when Spain took the gold and silver, "Latin American underdevelopment is the shadow of the North Atlantic development."[127] One of the favorite examples of the liberationists is the case of Chile. According to them, four North American copper companies took almost $11 billion dollars out of Chile in a period of 60 years, supposedly more than the gross national product for the country in its entire previous history of 400 years! [128]

---

[125] Martin H. Manser, ed., *The Westminster Collection of Christian Quotations* (Louisville, Kentucky: John Knox Press, 2001), p. 391.
[126] José Míguez Bonino, *Christians and Marxists*, p. 115.
[127] José Míguez Bonino, *La fe en busca de eficacia*, p. 39.
[128] McGovern, *Marxism*, pp. 211-215.

b. A Capitalist Answer

Michael Novak, in *The Spirit of Democratic Capitalism*, provides another perspective.[129] He says that it is not fair to blame only foreigners. Latin American poverty has existed for centuries, but the international economic exchange has been fairly low until recent years. In fact, the balance of interchange at times has favored Latin America. In 1850, the per capita income in Latin America was almost the same as in the United States. In 1892, the United States exported $96 million dollars to Latin America, while Latin America exported $290 million to the United States. Novak argues that if U.S. investment causes dependency and poverty, why has this not been the effect in Germany and Japan, for example, where the United States has invested as much or more than in Latin America? To answer the accusation that the United States has unjustly gained an enormous amount of money by investing in Latin America, he claims that they would have made more money by depositing the same amount in a bank in the United States!

What is the cause of Latin American poverty, then, according to Novak? He agrees that there have been abuses and injustices, both international and internal. However, he highlights other factors:

a) Population

In 1940, the population of Latin America was the same as in the United States: around 130 million. By 1977, the United States had 220 million, while Latin America had 342 million.

---

[129] Michael Novak, *The Spirit of Democratic Capitalism* (New York: Simon and Schuster, 1982), chapters 16, 17 y 18, pp. 272-314.

b) The Catholic Anti-Capitalist Mentality

In Europe, during the counter-reformation, the Catholic Church was closely tied to the government and discouraged capitalistic efforts. Capitalists left the Catholic countries and moved to Protestant countries, where they were successful. Catholic governments restricted private enterprise and gave license to the State monopolies. This occurred especially in countries that were dependent on Spain.

c) The Social Structure Imported from Spain

Furthermore, the Spanish exported the dualistic social structure to Latin America. A few people owned most of the land and the others worked for them. This system of owner/servant impeded freedom and discouraged private initiative. The situation was quite different in the early history of United States, where land was sold to many individual owners, and even given away on some occasions.

Novak argues that the economy is not so weak on the whole in Latin America, compared to other regions of the world. However, the distribution of income has been unequal.

Inflation

Inflation is one of the worst enemies of the economy. Often inflation is understood as simply an increase in prices. Nevertheless, inflation should be seen more precisely as a process by which money has less and less purchasing power. What is the cause?

Gary North is a reformed Christian economist, author of more than fifty books, known for his libertarian position. Although I do not share his extremist and theonomist position on law and politics, it seems to me that some of his comments on inflation make a lot of sense. He analyzes the following causes in his *Introduction to Christian Economics:*[130]

1) Weakening the metal in coins

North observes that in ancient Rome, when the government wanted to make more coins, instead of finding more gold or silver, they simply took some metal off the edge of the coins to make new ones. Today they do basically the same thing when they make "sandwich" coins (with silver on the faces and copper in between, for example), or when they change the metal completely (copper instead of gold, or nickel instead of silver). The result of this maneuver is that the coins are worth less, which is another form of inflation. Isaiah condemns Jerusalem for letting their silver become "dross" and for diluting their wine with water (Isaiah 1:21-22). [131]

2) Making money without backing of precious metals

Precious metals have intrinsic value because of their desirable beauty and their scarcity. Originally, most countries had gold to back paper bills. For every dollar bill, there was a piece of gold that was represented by the piece of paper. Then the governments began to print more bills than the gold in storage. If everyone tried to exchange their bills for gold now, there would not be enough.

Many countries dropped the gold standard in 1914, the year that World War I began.[132] The United States went back and forth until the Nixon administration, when they finally

---

[130] Gary North, *An Introduction to Christian Economics* (Nutley, N.J.: Craig Press, 1974).

[131] North, 3-18, 29-43.

[132] "Gold Standard," ed. Robert Whaples, *Economic History Association*, <http://eh.net/encyclopedia/article/officer.gold.standard> (Oct. 25, 2010).

abolished the gold standard altogether, and this has remained the situation until now.[133] North argues that this is the same as making counterfeit bills. The result is that every bill is worth less in the marketplace, which is inflation.[134]

Why does each bill buy less? Let's imagine a world in which there are 100-dollar bills in existence, 100 people in existence, and each person has one dollar. There are also 50 bottles of coca cola in existence, and they cost one dollar each. In this situation, 50 people could buy a coke, right? Nobody is excluded because they don't have enough money. If everyone wanted one, it would be a matter of selling one to the first 50 people who offer to buy one, or the first ones to get in line. Now let's suppose that the government decides to print 50 extra dollar bills, and they distribute one of them to each of 50 people. Now 50 people have two dollars, and 50 people only have one dollar. Again, let's suppose there are 50 bottles of coca cola for sale. If the salesperson is astute, he will realize that he is facing a good situation: he can raise the price of the cokes to two dollars and still sell all of them. Who will buy them? The people who have two dollars obviously have the advantage. The people who have only one dollar no longer have enough money to buy one. That is the way inflation works, according to North. Of course, this illustration is oversimplified, but it communicates the concept.

---

[133] See the following articles: Governor Ben S. Barnanke, "The Federal Reserve Board," <http://www.federalreserve.gov/BOARDDOCS/SPEECHES/2002/20021108/default.htm> (March 13, 2007), "The Gold Standard and the Great Depression," < <http://www.econbrowser.com/archives/2005/12/the_gold_standa.html>(March 13, 2007), and "Bretton Woods System," Wikipedia, <http://en.wikipedia.org/wiki/Bretton_Woods_system>(March 13, 2007).
[134] North, 6.

North explains that modern banking originated with the exchange of precious metal for paper notes, as far back as the Middle Ages. One could leave his coins with the banker, often a goldsmith, who gave him a receipt for his deposit. Soon the bankers realized that many people didn't come back for their coins before doing business, but instead they just exchanged the paper notes. This gave the bankers the opportunity to begin making loans, even loaning more than they were keeping. That is, there were many notes circulating "money" that didn't have enough coins to back them up. At that point, if everyone asked for their coins at once, the bank would go broke. The result is that the money has less buying power as it competes in the marketplace, just as we saw in the story of the cokes. Governments do the same thing today when they print bills (or make more money available electronically) without the backing of precious metals. The sad thing is that this inflation hurts the poor people most.[135]

3) The system of investments with interest ("fractional reserves")

Banks are also allowed to follow the pattern of the goldsmiths of the Middle Ages, in the sense that they are only required to keep a small percentage of the money deposited and can loan out the rest. This percentage may vary from time to time, and from country to country. The system is called "fractional-reserve banking." Let's suppose that the percentage is only 10%, which would not be uncommon (this was the required percentage in the United States in 2006).[136] This means that a person can deposit

---

[135] North, 21-22.
[136] Federal Reserve Bank of New York, "Reserve Requirements," (August 10, 2010) <http://www.newyorkfed.org/aboutthefed/fedpoint/fed45.html>.

$1,000, and theoretically, when the bank has finished handling this money, at the end almost $10,000 are in circulation. The result is again that each dollar has less competitive purchasing value in the marketplace. According to Gary North, this is a major cause of inflation.

The math is like this[137]:

Person # 1 has **$1,000** and deposits it all in the bank.
The bank keeps $100 and loans the rest ($900) to person # 2.

Person # 2 has **$900** and deposits it in another bank.
The bank keeps $90 and loans the rest ($810) to person # 3.

Person # 3 has **$810** and deposits it in another bank.
The bank keeps $ 81 and loans the rest ($729) to person # 4.

Person # 4 has **$729**, etc., etc.

If we continue this exercise ad infinitum (and we have not added the interest that the bank pays for the investments), the total amount of money that exists is about **$10,000**! Person #1 still has $1,000, #2 has $900, #3 has $891 etc. Notice that the money multiplied without doing hardly anything! The work involved was mainly that of the employees who handled the figures on the computer. The result: Even though person #1 thinks that he is earning money with the interest, there is ten times as much money in circulation, so each dollar has less purchasing power

---

[137] North, 32-33. North does this calculation, starting with $100. So does the article "Reserve Requirements" cited above.

(=inflation). It's like putting more and more water in the soup; each time it has less flavor. [138]

The capitalist system uses this process of credit and investment. Those who handle a lot of money make more, but the poor who have no money to invest lose the purchasing power of the little money they have.

The topic of fractional reserve banking has stimulated much debate. Not everyone would agree with Gary North. Some justify the system, saying that the money loaned by the bank is used to produce something and thus does not cause inflation. The principles of supply and demand also play an important role. For example, if a businessman borrows money to open a new bakery, there will be more bread available, and the greater supply will eventually lower the prices.

Following the same illustration of the cokes, let's suppose that there are now 100 cokes available instead of 50, and the government has printed extra bills so that 50 people have one dollar and 50 people have two dollars. No longer can the salesman charge two dollars for all of his cokes, because he will sell only 50 at that price. Furthermore, if people are simply not interested in cokes, the prices will remain low. Obviously, the real-life situation is more complex than our simplified explanation. However, a system that allows money to be multiplied so easily seems inherently faulty and unfair.

Prosperity Theology

There is currently a strong movement that has been called "prosperity theology," or "the prosperity gospel." The

---

[138] See also Wikipedia, "Fractional-reserve banking," <http://en.wikipedia.org/wiki/Fractional-reserve_banking> (March 13, 2007),

main postulate is that God blesses those who have sufficient faith materially and physically, in their finances and in their health. One Latin American survey reports that "the majority of Protestants in each country where the survey was conducted, from 56% in Brazil to 91% in Venezuela, express the belief that God provides material prosperity to the faithful."

This movement distorts biblical teaching. It is sufficient to look at the life of Jesus, Paul, and many faithful biblical characters who suffered persecution and poverty, not because of their lack of faith, but because God had a special purpose in it. It is true that we have biblical promises that one day we will lack nothing and we will never be sick (Revelation 21:1-4). However, this will not be until Christ returns to establish the eternal form of his kingdom. Just as the Jews had not understood that the Messiah would come in different stages, some Christians today are also confused, thinking that all the benefits of the Kingdom of God are experienced now. However, a more careful reading of the Bible teaches us that some promises have *already* been fulfilled (for example, we are forgiven and justified), others are *in process* (we are being sanctified), and others are *not yet* fulfilled (we do not have a new earth, renewed bodies, or total relief from the physical and spiritual effects of the Fall).

Economics in the Old Testament

We find three general ethical guidelines for economics highlighted in the Old Testament that should help us develop our economic philosophy: be honest, work diligently and show compassion.

The principle of honesty permeates the whole Old Testament. The ninth commandment is "You shall not bear false witness against your neighbor" (Exodus 20:16). Proverbs

11:1 says, "A false balance is an abomination to the Lord, but a just weight is His delight."

As we already saw in a previous chapter, the Pentateuch (in passages such as Leviticus 25) teaches us that we are free to make an effort to improve our situation, but that we must show compassion to the needy. There were many provisions made for the poor, such as leaving part of the crop unharvested so that they could find something to eat (Leviticus 23:22). Nobody should have starved to death in Israel! The story of manna in the desert (Exodus 16:16-31) illustrates several principles. Those who gathered much had just enough, and those who gathered little also had enough, which teaches us to avoid selfish excess and to care for those who have less. Those who tried to keep manna overnight found that it had gone bad by morning, which teaches us to trust God daily for our provision.

The Book of Proverbs emphasizes the wisdom of working hard and being honest (6:6-11, 16:11, 19:1, 20:4, 24:27, 26:13-14). Proverbs 30:8-9 teaches that it is better to be neither extremely wealthy nor extremely poor, because wealth tends to make us think we don't need God, but poverty tempts us to steal.

The prophets emphasize showing compassion and treating the needy with justice (Isaiah 3:14-15, Amos 2:6-7). These three ethical tones of honesty, diligence and compassion make a perfect harmony, and putting them into practice would establish a healthy and just economy.

Jesus and Economics

Just as we found in the previous chapter regarding politics, we find that Jesus did not make a statement about economic systems as we think of them today. However, He did inculcate new ethical values and new attitudes. We are not to lay up treasures on earth (Matthew 6:19-20), neither are we to be anxious about material things, but trust our heavenly Father (Matthew 6:25-34). Wealth can make it difficult to see the need for God, and therefore difficult to enter the Kingdom of God (Matthew 19:23). We should give to the poor, even be willing to give up everything if necessary (Luke 18:18-30). Jesus Himself gave us an example of leaving our comfort to help others.

2 Corinthians 8:9
For you know the grace of our Lord Jesus Christ, that though He was rich, yet for your sake He became poor, so that you through His poverty might become rich.

The Catholic Church, due to Liberation Theology, has adopted the notion that God has a "preferential love" for the poor.[139] I believe that if this refers only to those who are poor in the material sense, it is out of focus. But I agree that God has a special concern for those who are in need, whether it is someone who is depressed, who lives in a broken family, who is struggling with drugs or an alcoholic spouse, who lives far from home, or who is poor in material possessions. Those who are economically poor are not the only ones who suffer, and I believe that we should show special love to all of them, without considering anybody at all unworthy of our love. If we were to practice the values that Jesus left us, and if we were to have the attitude that Jesus had toward those who are suffering, the economy would be much better.

In Acts 2:44-5 and 4:32-7, it is evident that the church of the first century practiced the principles that Jesus had taught. They sold their possessions and shared with those in

---

[139] *Catechism of the Catholic Church*, paragraph # 2448

need, with the result that "there were no needy persons among them" (Acts 4:34). Some consider this a sort of "communist" experiment. However, the sharing was voluntary, the result of "much grace" being upon them (Acts 4:33). We see the same attitude in Paul, when he encourages the Corinthians to seek greater equality, following the guideline of the manna in the desert (2 Corinthians 8:14-15), but asks them to give out of grace, following the example of Christ, and not out of obligation (8:8-9).

The New Testament certainly doesn't encourage laziness or passivity. 2 Thessalonians 3:10 gives us a guideline: "If anyone is not willing to work, then he is not to eat either." But it does encourage us to be content with what we have. Paul says, "I know how to get along with humble means, and I also know how to live in prosperity" (Philippians 4:12; see also 1 Timothy 6:8 and Hebrews 13:5). I can testify to the fact that good relationships and a grateful attitude contribute more to happiness than material possessions.

Heinrich Böll writes a story about a happy fisherman and an annoying tourist. The fisherman had already gone to sea and had made his catch for the day, when a tourist comes along and wakes him from a nap with the clicking of his camera. They begin to talk, and the visitor tries to convince him that he should go back out again and catch more fish, in order to make more money and improve his business. The well-meaning visitor gets excited as he imagines how the poor man could eventually purchase more boats, build a factory, open a restaurant, and become very rich. "What then?", the unimpressed fisherman asks. "Then you may relax here in the harbor with your mind set at ease, doze in the sunshine and look out on the magnificent sea," the tourist argues. "But that is just what I am doing now!", says the fisherman.[140] This story illustrates the contrast between being eager to obtain more material possessions and learning to be content, an important lesson in our materialistic world.

Review Questions

1. How would you describe capitalism? What is the key value for capitalism?
2. Who wrote the classic defense of capitalism? What was his theory?
3. What do the critics of capitalism say about it, and what do the defenders say?
4. How would you describe socialism? What is the key value for socialism?
5. Who is considered the best-known proponent of socialism?
6. According to Marx, of what does the history of society fundamentally consist?
7. What did Marx say about religion?
8. How was the position of Marx and Engels different from that of Lenin regarding the way to bring about reform?
9. What is the difference between the extreme forms of socialism and the moderate forms?
10. What do the critics of socialism say about it, and what do the defenders say?
11. According to the author, what kind of economic system do we need?
12. What is the answer of Liberation Theology to the question of why Latin America is poor?

---

[140] Heinrich Böll, *Anekdote zur Senkung der Arbeitsmoral* ["Anecdote to the Decline of the Work Ethic"] There are many versions of this story, many without citing the source. For a translation by Hansjörg Bittner, see:
<http://www.uea.ac.uk/polopoly_fs/-
1.33246!np_vol_5_article_8_by_hansjorg_bittner.pdf > (August 11, 2010).

13. According to Michael Novak, what are the three most important causes of poverty in Latin America?

14. What are the causes of inflation, according to Gary North?

15. What is the main postulate of "prosperity theology"?

16. What are the three general ethical guidelines for economics that we find in the Old Testament?

17. What can we learn from Jesus about economics?

18. What can we learn from other passages of the New Testament about economics?

Questions for reflection

1. What do you think? Considering capitalism and socialism, which of the two systems best reflects Christian values?

2. What are some important biblical passages to give us guidelines to better manage the economy?

3. What is your opinion about why Latin America is poor, compared to Europe and the United States?

4. What are the economic problems in your country, and what solutions can you suggest?

5. What do you think of "prosperity theology"?

6. How has this lesson changed your perspective on economics? 7. What do you think of the Heinrich Böll story?

CHAPTER 7
TOWARD A CHRISTIAN VIEW OF SCIENCE AND MATHEMATICS

When I was in Junior High School, my science teacher said once that scientists should be the first ones to believe in God. He assured us that the more he studied nature, the more obvious it became that God existed. This is the way it should be. (Psalm 19:1: *The heavens declare the glory of God, and the sky above proclaims his handiwork.*)

Thankfully, science is an area in which even non-Christians tend to operate according to some valid presuppositions. For example, they assume the world is basically orderly and predictable, not chaotic. Furthermore, most scientists generally trust their ability to observe with their five senses and use their reasoning to draw conclusions. While we know that our abilities have been damaged by the Fall, man has not lost the ability to observe and reason.

Common grace (or "universal grace") reaches all mankind, making much scientific activity valid and beneficial. When my mother had heart problems, an excellent surgeon operated on her and saved her life. Even though he was not a Christian, and he was not even very friendly, I am very thankful for him. We should thank God for the discovery of medicines, for the analysis of physical and social problems, for the ability to predict the weather, and for the invention of so many things that make life more comfortable.

One important area where Christians should be cooperating with scientists is in the protection of our planet. When Francis Schaeffer wrote his book *Pollution and the Death of Man* in 1970[141], the topic was not as politicized as it

---

[141] Francis Schaeffer, *Pollution and the Death of Man* (Tyndale, 1970).

is now. I believe that current discussions have diverted us from a principle that was made clear in the first chapter of the Bible, that man has the task of caring for God's creation. They have distracted us from important issues such as taking care of our oceans and our air, and avoiding pollution in general. It's enough to arrive home with a blackened shirt collar after walking through the streets in the center of Santiago, Chile, or to see the dead fish floating among the plastic remains on the coasts of Florida, to know that man is damaging the environment. We should be careful not to let our hesitant attitude toward science lead us to be on the wrong side of this issue. We don't have to agree with everything scientists say to cooperate with them on something as important as caring for the planet, something that affects all of humanity.[142] [143] If I live in a condo building that needs repairs to prevent a collapse or a fire, I don't have to agree with all the religious or political beliefs of the other residents to cooperate with them in efforts to save the building!

However, we have to recognize that an intellectual conflict has unfortunately developed between science and Christianity in the last centuries. This is due to the fact that much science has become independent of faith. In order to be "objective," scientists tend to leave God outside the classroom when they study biology, chemistry, physics, or psychology.

---

[142] Katherine Hayhoe, *Saving Us; A Climate Scientist's Case for Hope and Healing in a Divided World*. (New York: One Signal Publishers/Atria Books, 2021), p. 6. The author serves as the climate ambassador for the *World Evangelical Alliance*.
[143] John Copeland Nagle, "The Evangelical Debate Over Climate Change," U. St. Thomas L.J. 53 (2008). <https://scholarship.law.nd.edu/law_faculty_scholarship/433>

Intellectual Integrity

The Conflict

Christians accept two sources of revelation: nature, and the Scriptures. Since God is the author of both forms of revelation, they do not contradict each other. Therefore, when we practice science correctly and study the Bible correctly, there is no conflict. Nevertheless, there are apparent contradictions caused by erroneous interpretations, either of the Bible or of nature. For example, the theory of evolution is an apparent contradiction between the Bible and scientific evidence. Also, some psychological theories do not coincide with the biblical teaching about man, about guilt, and about sin. Such topics force us to distinguish the Christian view of science from non-Christian perspectives.

Our relationship with science has been further complicated in the last centuries because of a tendency to separate faith and reason. We mentioned Kant previously, who highlighted this separation. The problem is that science is often considered reasonable and objective, as opposed to religious matters, which seem ambiguous and unknowable.

Dr. H. van Riessen of the *Free University of Amsterdam* reminds us that the reformers tried to encourage the development of the sciences in order to serve God, and that they opposed a separation of science and faith. It was humanism that repressed this effort and left science as autonomous. He says, "The cause of the crisis is man's belief in his own independent strength and in his own dominion over the world by means of science."[144]

We should give Scripture the priority when we carry out intellectual tasks like trying to harmonize science and the

---

[144] Van Riesen, *Enfoque cristiano de la Ciencia* [A Christian View of Science] (Barcelona: Fundación Editorial de Literatura Reformada, 1973) p. 28.

Bible. It's not that one form of revelation, the Bible or nature, is better than the other; they are different. Both come from God Himself, and we need the guidance of the Holy Spirit to understand both. But we need Scripture to interpret nature more than we need nature to interpret Scripture, because nature can be more easily misunderstood. The Bible is verbal revelation and thus can communicate more directly and precisely to the human intellect. A beautiful sunset might communicate a wide variety of things to people, but when we read, "Now the time came for Elizabeth to give birth, and she bore a son" (Luke 1:57), it communicates the same historical fact clearly to all of us.

It's like the illustration we mentioned previously of a survivor from a shipwreck.[145] He wakes up on the shore and finds objects from the ship such as coins, a compass, and clothes, but he needs help to understand what has happened. In the same way, creation reveals many things to us, but we need the Scriptures to understand them better. Reading the Bible is like reading the captain's diary.

The Theory of Evolution

One of the greatest challenges for the Christian faith has been the atheistic version of the theory of evolution. The evolutionistic perspective has had an enormous influence, not only in the realm of science, but also in philosophy (the dialectic of Hegel), economics (Marx), religion (Teilhard de Chardin), linguistics (all languages evolved from a mother language), and almost every realm of thought. Some suppose that not only the material world, but also the world of man's thought, has been constantly evolving toward something better.

---

[145] Philip Yancey, *Soul Survivor; How My Soul Survived the Church*, pp. 51-52.

Intellectual Integrity

This perspective has caused many to doubt the Christian faith, because it pretends to explain the existence of everything without God. R. Albert Mohler Jr. notes that "Darwin's theory of natural selection and the larger dogma of evolution emerged in the nineteenth century as the first coherent alternative to the Bible's doctrine of creation." He quotes biologist Richard Dawkins as saying, "Darwin made it possible to be an intellectually fulfilled atheist." Mohler talks about the "new atheism" and says people like Dawkins have become even more bold and antagonistic, now claiming that evolution makes it "impossible" to be an intellectually fulfilled Christian. [146]

However, this Issue should not be a stumbling block for the Christian faith. The Bible clearly teaches that God made all things miraculously by the power of His Word. ("By faith we understand that the universe was created by the word of God, so that what is seen was not made out of things that are visible." Hebrews 11:3). But there are various ways to seek harmony between the scientific evidence used in defense of the theory of evolution and the Biblical account of creation. I am not a scientist, and the more I read about this subject, the more I realize I shouldn't be dogmatic about my view. However, this doesn't mean I shouldn't try to come to a tentative conclusion.

Options

We'll take a look at some options, beginning with a brief summary of the perspectives presented in *Four Views on Creation, Evolution, and Intelligent Design*.[147]

---

[146] Dockery, David S; Wax, Trevin. *Christian Worldview Handbook* (p. 168-169). B&H Publishing Group. Kindle Edition. Mohler's article is "The New Atheism."

[147] *Four Views on Creation, Evolution, and Intelligent Design*. Copyright © 2017 by Ken Ham, Hugh Ross, Deborah B. Haarsma, Stephen C. Meyer, J. B. Stump.

1. Young earth creationism (Ken Ham)

This view is that God created the earth and universe already mature, with the appearance of having existed for millions or billions of years. Adam was created as an adult, and not a newborn baby. The trees and other plants were also created grown, and the same would apply to all of creation. Everything was made already mature with the appearance of age.

Ken Ham focuses first on Scripture, arguing that Genesis 1 is history and that the days are 24-hour days.[148] He believes that the global catastrophe caused by the great flood explains the existence of fossils and sedimentary rock layers that give the impression of an old earth.[149] He adds that there are some logical problems with an evolutionary scheme of millions of years. For example, how could plants survive without animals and insects to pollinate them?[150]

2. Old earth creationism (Hugh Ross), also called the "day-age" perspective.

According to this perspective, each "day" of Genesis 1 represents a span of many years, in which God periodically introduced new species, progressing from simple to complex. As He did, He also adapted everything to be in harmony, in "optimal ecological relationships."[151] Adam and Eve were the first humans, not descendants of apes. Hugh Ross appeals to verses such as Psalm 90:4 and 2 Peter 3:8 (...with the Lord

---

Zondervan (Counterpoints: Bible and Theology). Zondervan Academic. Kindle Edition.

[148] *Four Views*, p. 20.

[149] *Four Views*, pp 27-29.

[150] *Four Views*, p. 22. See also: Q&A: What is Young Earth Creationism (YEC)? (thirdmill.org)

[151] *Four Views*, pp. 71-73.

one day is as a thousand years, and a thousand years as one day.") to show that in the Bible, a "day" does not always refer to a 24-hour period of time.[152]

3. Evolutionary creation (Deborah Haarsma), also called "theistic evolution."

According to this school of thought, God governed the process of gradual evolution to produce the diverse life forms over billions of years. Deborah Haarsma appeals to important figures such as B. B. Warfield and Billy Graham who were at least open to this view. She argues that the layers of ice in the Antarctic point to an age of 700,000 years and the layers of sedimentary rock in lakes and oceans point to millions of years. She also finds radiometric dating proof of an age of billions of years in rock formations in places like Greenland. This process measures time by the amount of decay that has occurred in radioactive atoms.[153]

Haarsma makes the following comment:

> First, how do we know that God didn't simply create everything six thousand years ago but made it appear billions of years old? The short answer is, we don't. There is no scientific way to tell the difference between an ancient universe and one that was made to look in every detail as though it were ancient. Yet there is a profound spiritual difference. Scripture is clear in teaching that God is a God of truth and that the heavens declare his glory. God's activity in the natural world speaks to us just as truly as his words in Scripture, and we must take it seriously.[154]

---

[152] *Four Views,* p. 80. See also: Q&A: What is the Day Age Theory? (thirdmill.org)
[153] *Four Views,* pp.134-136.
[154] *Four Views,* p. 134

4. Intelligent Design (Stephen C. Meyer)

This option is not exactly another position regarding how to harmonize the scientific evidence with the biblical account of creation. All positions that believe in creation also believe that nature points to intelligent design. However, some who identify with this category actually prefer not to even make a pronouncement regarding the biblical account. Stephen C. Meyer says:

> ...The theory of intelligent design does not offer an interpretation of the book of Genesis, nor does it posit a theory about the length of the biblical days of creation or the age of the earth. Consequently, intelligent design proponents may have a variety of positions on such issues (or none at all).
>
> ... The theory of intelligent design holds that there are telltale features of living systems and the universe—for example, the digital code in DNA, the miniature circuits and machines in cells, and the fine tuning of the laws and constants of physics—that are best explained by an intelligent cause rather than an undirected material process.[155]

We could add some other views besides the ones proposed in the book *Four Views*.

5. The Gap Theory

A fifth view is that there was a long period of time (a "gap") between the initial creation of Genesis 1:1 and the days described in Genesis 1:3-31. Verse two says, "The earth

---

[155] *Four Views*, pp. 179-180.

was without form and void," which they argue could be translated, "But earth *became* without form and void." According to this theory, the original creation became corrupt and was destroyed in order to start over. This view became popular partly because of notes in the Scofield Reference Bible.[156]

6. The Framework Theory

Another view is that the creation account in chapter one of Genesis is not giving us a chronology of events, but rather a "framework" of creation, in which the first three days define realms, and days four to six describe what fills these realms. It is meant to be read poetically, not historically. This perspective could allow for a variety of ways to harmonize the biblical account with scientific theories. It has been promoted by theologians such as Meredith Kline and Bruce Waltke.[157]

Questions

Most of these options raise some important questions. First, for any view that interprets Genesis 1 and 2 as poetic and not historical, how do they explain so many details that sound very much like historical details? For example, the passage repeats over and over, "God said...", and then it came to be. Also, for every day it says, "And there was evening and there was morning, the ___ day." The narration of the creation of Adam and Eve includes important specific details. Adam was made from the dust of the ground, in God's image, and God breathed into him the "breath of life," then commanded him to take care of the garden. God said it

---

[156] The Gap Theory (Part A) | Answers in Genesis
[157] Q&A: The Framework Theory (thirdmill.org)

was not good for him to be alone, then He made Eve. Furthermore, the story of their sinful disobedience and the Fall are an essential part of redemptive history as taught in all of Scripture, and it assumes they were real historical people.

Secondly, is there sufficient fossil evidence of transitional forms to support the perspective of a gradual evolutionary process? Some say no.[158] Ken Ham quotes Harvard evolutionist Stephen Gould as saying:

> The extreme rarity of transitional forms in the fossil record persists as the trade secret of paleontology. The evolutionary trees that adorn our textbooks have data only at the tips and nodes of their branches; the rest is inference, however reasonable, not the evidence of fossils.[159]

Others insist that the fossil record is sufficient to prove gradual evolution. Deborah Haarsma says, "What was once a gap in the fossil record has been filled by many species in recent decades." For example, she claims there are more than a thousand fossil specimens that support the gradual evolution of the whale, beginning with wolf-like land creatures. She also asserts that there are fossils of over six thousand individual creatures of several species showing a gradual transition from apes to homo sapiens during a period of several million years.[160]

---

[158] Duane Gish, *Evolution: The Challenge of the Fossil Record* (San Diego: Master Books Pub., 1985), p. 33 in the Spanish version, *Creación, evolución y el registro fósil* (Barcelona: CLIE, 1979).

[159] *Four Views*, p. 156.

[160] Four views, pp. 140, 145.

Gould has proposed a new version of evolution called "punctuated equilibrium." According to this version of the evolutionary theory, the species maintained an equilibrium during long periods of time and then experienced sudden changes.[161] This would fit the scheme of the day-age view.

Thirdly, while the day-age view is tempting, why does the order of the creation stages in Genesis not coincide with the order proposed by evolutionists? For example, the Genesis account states that the birds were created before land animals (days 5 and 6), while most evolutionists would turn the order around. There is also a question of why there would be death before the Fall. Wasn't death part of the curse caused by the Fall? Some would answer that the death caused by the Fall only refers to man, or maybe it refers to spiritual death.[162]

Fourthly, how do old-earth views #2 (day-age), #3 (divinely guided evolution), and #6 (framework) explain the fact that homo sapiens supposedly existed long before Adam and Eve? Why doesn't the Bible mention this? In fact, Genesis seems to indicate clearly that Adam and Eve were the first human beings. I suppose they might answer that the examples that evolutionists consider homo sapiens were not really human beings.

In the fifth place, the gap theory raises the question of corruption before the Fall. Why did everything go bad? It also seems to force an unusual interpretation of Genesis 1:2, and the rest of chapter 1 for that matter. The account seems to indicate that God created the light and plants and animals for the first time in those six days.

---

[161] Stephen Jay Gould, *The Structure of Evolutionary Theory* (Cambridge, MA: Harvard University Press, 2002), 745ff.

[162] Evolution vs. Creation: The Order of Events Matters! | Answers in Genesis

Finally, the young earth view may make us wonder why God would do things that way. It seems like it is deceitful to some people, leaving evidence that is confusing. However, the great flood might explain a lot of things.

Tentative Conclusion

While none of the options is without doubts, the view that seems to have fewer problems is the young earth view. It would be hard to prove that it *didn't* happen that way. As Deborah Haarsma admits, "How do we know that God didn't simply create everything six thousand years ago but made it appear billions of years old? The short answer is, we don't."

It's especially important to maintain the direct and miraculous creation of Adam and Eve. John Frame says:

> God created us directly by a special act. That implies that we are not the descendants of animals; we are not "evolved." God made the man Adam from dirt, and the dirt did not come alive until God breathed in the breath that made him man. Genesis 2:7 does not say that God made an animal out of the dirt and later turned the animal into a man, but that God made a man right there on the spot, out of the dirt. Even more obviously, God made the woman by a miraculous act in Genesis 2:21-22.[163]

The young earth view seems to make sense when you consider how all of creation is interdependent. Spanish biologist and theologian Antonio Cruz speaks of "irreducible

---

[163] John M. Frame. *Salvation Belongs to the Lord: An Introduction to Systematic Theology* (Kindle Locations 1086-1089). Kindle Edition.

complexity," giving credit to Michael Behe for the concept. This means that some things are so complex that they don't function unless they are totally developed. The eye is a good example. It won't function without the nerve, the retina, and the pupil being completely developed. [164]

This same concept can be applied to nature as a whole. Many things depend on each other to function properly. In fact, the whole natural system is delicately interdependent. When a species is in danger of extinction, scientists point out that to lose one species may affect many others. For example, we can't live without bees to pollinate plants. This principle makes it easy to believe that God would have made all of creation in a mature and developed state, and that He would have made everything near the same time.

Whitcomb and Morris observe that plants need chemicals that normally come from a long process of decomposition and erosion. Therefore, the first plants would have been nourished from soil that had the appearance of age.[165]

These two authors were some of the earliest to combine the young earth interpretation with an analysis of the effects of the Great Flood. They think that the flood brought a drastic change in the climate, with a sudden cooling and the formation of ice in some places, causing the sudden death of large animals like dinosaurs and mammoths. It would have also caused the glaciers to slide, forming valleys and canyons

---

[164] Antonio Cruz, *Sociología; una desmitificación*, pp. 210-214. [Sociology; a demythologization] See also See Michael J. Behe, William A. Dembski, and Stephen C. Meyer, *Science and Evidence for Design in the Universe* (San Francisco: Ignatius Press, 2000).

[165] John C. Whitcomb, Jr. y Henry M. Morris, *The Genesis Flood; The Biblical Record and Its Scientific Implications* (Nutley, New Jersey: Presbyterian and Reformed Publishing Company, 1961), pp. 232-233. Whitcomb is professor of Old Testament (Th.D.) and Morris is a scientist, director of the Institute of Creation Research (Ph.D.).

that look like they are the result of a long process. They believe that the Flood produced not only rain, but also earthquakes and volcanic eruptions. Genesis 7:11 points to other catastrophic events at the time of the Flood, besides the heavy rain: "the springs of the great deep burst forth".[166]

Think about this: What "age" did Adam have in the moment he was created? Did he have the body of a thirty-year-old man? Possibly. At least he was not a new-born baby. So if you had arrived one minute after his creation, how would you calculate the time of his creation? The evidence might make you think that he had been created years previously, right? Think also of the plants and trees. Adam and Eve needed food, so God would have given them plants already grown with fruits and vegetables, not just seeds. Again, suppose that you arrive one minute after the creation of the plants and you begin to examine a tree to see how old it is. You cut the trunk of the tree, count the rings, and you might conclude that it has been growing for hundreds of years, while in reality it has existed for only one minute. And if God did this with Adam and Eve and the trees, He probably did it with everything else. Is this deceitful on God's part? No! It would be totally appropriate.

This interpretation that God made all things with the appearance of age seems to coincide best with the biblical account, and it avoids some of the problems that other views face. It also seems to be supported by the concept of irreducible complexity and interdependence. Anything that seems to show evidence of a very old earth can be explained by the mature creation approach and by the effects of the Great Flood. However, I still believe we should not be dogmatic about this. The subject is very complicated and

---

[166] Whitcomb y Morris, *The Genesis Flood*, pp. 258-281.

requires an enormous amount of study. Again, the important thing is that we can agree that "By faith we understand that the universe was created by the word of God, so that what is seen was not made out of things that are visible." (Hebrews 11:3)

The Place of the Bible in Science

The Bible is not a scientific textbook. However, when it speaks of scientific facts, it tells the *truth*. It is not separated from science, or contrary to science. It gives a basis for science. It doesn't necessarily give specific verses to answer many of our questions, but it provides a foundation.

What should we do when there are apparent conflicts between science and the Bible? We should begin with the conviction that God does not contradict himself, and that there is no real conflict between evidence in nature and the Bible. Therefore, when we see apparent contradictions, we should study the Bible again and check our scientific research, seeking harmony. It's possible that we might never find the final answer sometimes, and some biblical data such as dates and numbers may seem imprecise to our contemporary mind, but we know that there were no errors in the original inspired documents. There is always agreement between God's revelation in nature and God's revelation in the Scriptures, whether we understand it properly or not.

Mathematics

Supposedly mathematics is a "neutral" field of thought, and supposedly there is no difference between the Christian view and an atheistic view. Normally, we see little difference because even non-Christians function in this field on the basis of a trust in logic and an orderly universe. However, there are examples of differences.

Vern Poythress presents us with some examples of how philosophical presuppositions influence in mathematics. There are "intuitionist" mathematicians (L.E.J. Brouwer and Arend Heyting) that do not accept arguments by *reductio ad absurdum* (proving something by showing that its denial produces a contradiction). For example, let's look at the supposition that there is only one straight line between two points. The intuitionists say that we cannot be sure of this, since it can only be proven by *reductio ad adsurdum*. Something as important as π (pi), used for example to calculate the area of a circle ($A = \pi r^2$), is a controversial subject. Since it is an infinite number, some question the validity of its existence. On the other hand, Christians say that God knows the true value of π, and therefore we can speak legitimately of its existence.[167]

A person who believes that the world was formed by chance and disorder would have problems explaining why the world corresponds so well with mathematics. However, the Christian knows that the world was made in an orderly fashion by God. The intelligent design includes physical laws that are in harmony with the logic of mathematics.

Poythress proposes several Christian presuppositions for doing mathematics:

1) All knowledge comes from the mind of God.
2) There is unity and plurality in the universe. This has its origin and its explanation in the Triune God, who is three in one.
3) God knows everything, and therefore we can talk about things such as infinity and π.

---

[167] *Foundations of Christian Scholarship*, pp. 159-190.

4) Man is the image of God. Therefore, he has the capacity of *a priori* mathematic thought, as well as the capacity to examine the world *a posteriori*.
5) God made everything with order. Mathematical structures are not part of the creation, but they reflect the nature of God in the creation.

Jesus and science

It is difficult to think of Bible passages where Jesus says something specifically about science as we understand it today. Nevertheless, we shouldn't forget that Jesus participated in the miracle of creation (Hebrews 1:2). This means that all of creation reflects His nature. We can't clearly understand the gospel from creation alone, but it contains symbols and hints of spiritual truths. Jesus illustrated many spiritual truths with objects of nature, such as seeds, trees, vines, wheat, flowers, and birds.

It's important to recognize that Jesus also showed that the universe is not "closed," as some philosophers and scientists would have us believe. In fact, His very incarnation was a way of breaking through the barriers of the universe. Each miracle that He performed shows that He is sovereign, and that He is above the normal functions of creation. He can break the patterns that He Himself established whenever He wants. In fact, nature depends on Him at every moment. As it says in Hebrews 1:3, He "upholds all things by the Word of His power."

The wise men who went to see the baby Jesus were probably religious men who studied astrology. The fact that they came from foreign lands to worship Jesus symbolizes the proper posture of all science: kneeling before Jesus.

Review Questions

1. What are some valid presuppositions that even non-Christians use in their scientific activities?

2. What makes much scientific activity valid and beneficial for all of humanity?

3. What is the cause of the conflict between science and Christianity in the last centuries?

4. Why should there not be a conflict between science and Christianity?

5. Explain possible ways to harmonize the biblical account of creation with the apparent age of the earth and the evidence that evolutionists present.

6. What are some of the key questions related to each of the possible explanations?

7. Explain the author's suggested view.

8. Explain the concept of "irreducible complexity" and its importance in considering the theory of the creation of a mature earth with the appearance of old age.

9. What should we do when there are apparent conflicts between science and the Bible?

10. Why do "intuitionist" mathematicians say that we cannot confirm with certainty that there is only one straight line between two points and that we cannot speak of the validity of the value of "π"?

11. According to Vern Poythress, why does man have the capacity of *a priori* mathematic thought, as well as the capacity to examine the world *a posteriori*?

12. Why does all nature teach us something of Jesus?

13. What is the symbolism in the fact that the wise men went to worship Jesus?

Intellectual Integrity

Questions for reflection

1. What should our attitude be toward science?
2. What is your theory about harmonizing the biblical account of creation with the apparent old age of the earth?
3. Do you believe that there is much difference between the way in which a Christian does mathematics and the way in which a non-Christian does it? Why or why not?
4. Can you think of other biblical teachings about Jesus' relation to science?

CHAPTER 8
TOWARD A CHRISTIAN VIEW OF THE ARTS

Art is one of the most important aspects of a Christian worldview. Christians should be more interested in art than anybody. For one thing, as we analyze art, we can detect the philosophical, psychological, and spiritual condition of society. Since artists tend to be sensitive and spiritually profound, they frequently understand problems more intuitively, and they express their concerns in their art. Painters, sculptors, musicians, and writers are like *cultural prophets*. Makoto Fujimura calls artists "border-stalkers" who are "often found at the margins of society, meandering into the borders of established thought patterns."[168] Artists not only detect changes; they actually participate in shaping culture.

Secondly, we can see God's image in their creativity. When a person produces art, he or she is reflecting something of God. This should also motivate Christians to use their artistic gifts.

Finally, we should be able to enjoy art as a gracious gift from God. What would life be like without music, art, and literature? It would be like a boring diet of bread and water. Fujimura tells the story of when he and his wife were newly married and struggling to make ends meet. When his wife came home with flowers, he scolded her saying, "How could you think of buying flowers if we can't even eat!" Her answer was, "We need to feed our souls, too."[169] Art feeds our souls.

---

[168] Fujimura, *Art and Faith*, pp. 15, 46. Kindle edition.
[169] Makoto Fujimura, *Culture Care* (Downers Grove, IL: IVP, 2017), location 133. Kindle Edition.

However, Evangelicals sometimes tend to shy away from the arts. Why? Partly because they see them as unwholesome, sometimes even hostile to Christianity. I know people who read only books written by Christians. Others threw away all the books and music they had when they were converted, because somebody made them think they were bad for them. Like science, art should be our friend, but sometimes it doesn't seem that way.

The Secularization of Art

Throughout long periods of European history, art was predominantly a channel of Christian expression. It's obvious when you walk through an art museum like the *Louvre* in chronological order, or when you read a book on the history of art. As I leaf through *A History of Art* by H. W. Janson, I see that Christian themes dominated painting and sculpture from the time of Constantine in the fourth century through the time of the Renaissance (around 1600). [170]

Then when I look at the chapter on the "Baroque in Italy and Germany" (starting in 1600), I begin to see more secular scenes. In the section on the "modern world" (starting in 1750), the change is even more notable. There are very few religious themes, but many landscapes, scenes of typical daily life, and portraits of common people. *The Maids of Honor* by Diego Velasquez (1656) replaces *The Last Supper* by Leonardo Da Vinci (1495-98), and the execution scene in *The Third of May, 1808* by Francisco Goya (painted in 1814-15) replaces *The Crucifixion* by Jan Van Eyck (1420-25).

We could trace a similar change in music. Beginning with the *Gregorian Chant* in the sixth or seventh century, sacred

---

[170] H. W. Janson, *A History of Art* (Englewood Cliffs, N.J.: Prentice-Hall, 1969.

music dominated Europe throughout the Middle Ages. Then secular music became more popular during the Renaissance. However, in this case, even during the baroque and classical periods, some of the most famous composers of all history, such as Johann Sebastian Bach (1685-1750), George Frideric Handel (1685-1759), and Franz Joseph Haydn (1732-1809), composed much of their music with Christian themes. Even Ludwig Van Beethoven (1770-1827) composed some masses, although his personal religious views were not clear.[171] From here on, the secular influence has been stronger.

Literature during the Middle Ages in Europe was mostly dedicated to the discussion of matters of faith. Dante (1265-1321) and Chaucer (1343-1400) even wrote fiction based on Christian themes. The printing press, invented in the middle of the fifteenth century, was used for printing the Bible and religious literature. Then, as with other cultural activity, the Renaissance and the modern period brought a tendency toward secularization..

In his fascinating book, *Modern Art and the Death of a Culture*,[172] H. R. Rookmaaker analyzes the message of many works of art, from the Middle Ages to the twentieth century. He argues that modern art communicates the end of an age, an age when man trusted reason and the truth. According to Rookmaaker, the reformers gave little attention to the fine arts and did not produce their own style of art, with the exception of the first half of the seventeenth century in Holland (Rembrandt, 1606-1669).[173] This vacuum was due to what he calls Protestant "mysticism," especially evident among the Puritans, a tendency to emphasize subjective

---

[171] "Music History 102," http://www.ipl.org/div/mushist/ (Sept. 9, 2010).
[172] H.R. Rookmaaker, *Modern Art and the Death of a Culture* (Downers Grove, Illinois: Inter-Varsity Press, 1970).
[173] Rookmaaker, pp. 29-31.

spirituality and avoid "worldly" pursuits. At the same time, the Roman Catholic tendency was to separate the realms of the spiritual and the natural, of faith and reason, leaving the arts independent of spiritual influence.[174] Both of these attitudes left humanism as the dominant factor in culture. However, the humanist emphasis on secularized science led man to feel trapped in a "closed box."[175]

Modern art shows his attempt to get out of that box. The first step toward modern art was *realism*. The realists painted nothing but the objective "facts" (Goya). The second step toward modern art was *impressionism*. They painted what they perceived, but instead of painting it as objective facts, they represented their own subjective impressions (Renoir). The last steps of modern art were *expressionism* and the *dada* movement. The expressionists painted, not the facts, nor their impressions of what they observed, but what they wanted to express (Picasso). According to the dada movement, life has no meaning. They laugh at everything of value. They way they found a name for the movement says a lot: they opened a French dictionary randomly and pointed to any word. The finger landed on "dada", which means "rocking horse."

In the twentieth century, culture "dies," according to Rookmaaker. He quotes Karel Appel saying, "I don't paint. I hit. Painting is destruction." Francis Bacon paints the head of a man screaming from inside a box, and writes, "Now...man is conscious of the fact that he is an accident, that he is completely useless, and that he must finish the game with no reason."[176] While Rookmaaker did not use the term, he was speaking of what we now call "Postmodernism."

---

[174] Rookmaaker, pp. 34-35.
[175] Rookmaaker, p. 47.
[176] Rookmaaker, p. 174.

How can we describe postmodern art? It's difficult because it includes such a wide variety of styles. I think the best word to use is "eclectic."[177] Douglas Groothuis says, "Postmodern pluralism has produced a great profusion of styles and forms, with no coherence in sight." He argues that postmodernists consider art an expression of subjective personal tastes, not an expression of absolute truth or of values that can be evaluated objectively. [178]

The postmodern mentality is often manifested in the lyrics of styles of music such as *alternative music* and *heavy metal*. For example, look at the words to the following song "Plain" by a group called "311." The phrase "tabla rosa" makes reference to the empiricist philosophical idea that our mind is a blank slate, with nothing written on it. *Yin* and *Yang* are religious terms in Chinese religion, referring to good and evil, which according to them are only apparently opposites, while in reality they are one and the same. Notice that, if there are no absolutes, you can't distinguish between good and evil, not even between God and the devil!

> Tabla Rosa is my brain
> don't have to guess just what I'm sayin'
> don't mean to bug or drive you insane
> if I had a point I'd say it plain
> oh, dammit my brain is blank
> ...
> Don't you know the devil is in me and God she is too
> my Yin hits my Yang But what the heck ya gonna do
> I choose a rocky ass path but that's how I like it

---

[177] Karen Wright, "Born in a Balloon," *Modern Painters; Special American Issue*, Fall, 2002, p. 19.
[178] Douglas Groothuis, *Truth Decay* (Downers Grove, Illinois: InterVarsity Press, 2000), p. 245.

life's a bowl of punch go ahead and spike it.[179]

This helps us understand a new tendency during recent decades, but it would be a distortion to suggest that the majority of contemporary musicians represent postmodernism. There will always be songs about love, songs with a rhythm for dancing, and protest songs, for example. An interesting video of a moving timeline shows the best-selling music artists world-wide from 1969-2019:[180]

Another similar video shows the most popular genres of music worldwide from 1910-2019.[181] The following list shows the #1 style for each period:

1910-11 Opera
1912 Marches
1913-15 Opera (again)
1916-33 Country
1934 Jazz
1945-52 Country (again)
1953-55 R&B
1956-59 Rock and Roll (jumps quickly after starting in 1955)
1960-71 Soul
1972 Pop Rock
1973-79 Disco
1980 Pop Rock

---

[179] 311, "Plain," Internet site: <ttp://www.azlyrics.com/lyrics/311/plain.html> (June 1, 2010).

[180] Best-Selling Music Artists 1969-2019 < https://youtu.be/a3w8I8boc_I> It says: "...ranked by yearly certified record sales. Numbers are worldwide and adjusted to twelve months trailing average. Recent years data includes digital singles sales as reported by online music retailers and streaming services."

[181] "Most Popular Music Styles 1910-2019" < https://youtu.be/eP88FUL7d_8> Sept. 9, 2021. It says, "Historical popularity is based on worldwide vinyl and CD records release frequencies for specific genre adjusted to recent years' music charts."

1981-86 Techno Pop
1987-88 Pop Rock (again)
1989-2008 House
2009-2019 Hip-hop / Rap

In 2019, the top 11 styles were in the following order: Hip-hop/Rap, Techno, R&B, Punk, Alternative Rock, House, Country, Indie-rock, Electro, Latin, Techno-pop.

Some Christians are making an impact through popular styles of music. For example, Bono, who openly declares himself to be a Christian, is still one of the most famous rock musicians. Christianity Today writes about rappers such as Lecrae and Shai Linne, saying that "their lyrics proclaim the gospel through a music style long known for addressing raw truths and the fallen state of society."[182]

Evaluating Art

Let's look at a few examples of authors who encourage us to develop a Christian view of art and suggest guidelines for evaluating art.

H. R. Rookmaaker

In *Art Needs no Justification*,[183] Rookmaaker explains that art has useful functions, but argues that these are not what gives it value. Art has its own value because of its beauty. He gives an illustration of a tree, which has many useful purposes: it produces shade, oxygen, and wood, for example. But its major importance is in being part of the creation. God gave humanity the capacity to do many artistic things, such as music, poetry, decorations, and sculptures.

---

[182] "Hip Hop," *Christianity Today* online, May 2013. <www.christianitytoday.com>
[183] Rookmaaker, *Art Needs No Justification* (Downers Grove, Illinois: InterVarsity Press, 1978.)

The simple fact of using these capacities already pleases God, even though we may not always see any practical utility to them, because they are a way of giving back a gift to God. Therefore, art needs no justification. Art has its own value and should be appreciated simply as beauty.

Dorothy Sayers

In *The Whimsical Christian*, author Dorothy Sayers writes a chapter called "Toward a Christian Aesthetic." She says that a work of art is something new, not just a copy. It is a "creation," using materials that God already created, but applying personal creativity, which is part of the image of God in man. Just as God made man in His image, man also makes art in his "image." That is, the art reflects something of the artist and his character. It is not that the poet says, "Oh, how beautiful the moon is! I'll try to find words to express what people should think of the moon!" Rather the writer finds himself saying words in his head and when he writes them down and reads them, he says to himself, "That's it! That is what the experience of seeing the moon was for me! Now I recognize it and know what it was!" It involves his experience, his expression of the experience, and the recognition of the validity of that expression. Art contains something of what the artist perceives, but it also contains something of himself. Sayers argues that "art" that is only made to entertain is not really art, but a falsification. There is no problem with doing something once in a while to entertain, but it should not replace true art.[184]

---

[184] Dorothy Sayers, *The Whimsical Christian; 18 essays* (New York: Collier, 1978). Also published by the title, *Christian Letters to a Post-Christian World* (New York: Collier, 1987).

Francis Schaeffer

Schaeffer did much to renew interest in art among Evangelicals. In *Art and the Bible*,[185] he highlights the fact that Christ redeemed the whole man and that Christ is the Lord of every aspect of life. He shows that art had a place in the Bible, for example in the construction of the tabernacle (Exodus 25-28) and the temple (2 Chronicles 3-4). The Bible contains beautiful poetry and lovely songs. The Psalms encourage us to glorify God with dance and with musical instruments (Psalms 149 and 150). Schaeffer insists that art has value in itself, just for its own beauty, and not necessarily for its "usefulness." He challenges us to make a work of art out of our own lives.

He recommends four guidelines for evaluating art.
a. Technical excellence. (Is it done well?)
b. Validity (Was it done in harmony with the worldview of the artist?)
c. Intellectual content. (Is its message or worldview true?)
d. Integrity (Are the content and form of communication in harmony?)

Let's try to apply these principles to a song that was popular a few years ago. Look below at the words to "Toxicity" by a group called *System of a Down*. Notice that the phrases seem to have meaning, but the song as a whole is fragmented and incoherent. They seem to be protesting some kind of corruption. I suppose they wanted to communicate the idea that life is disorder, and therefore the lyrics of the song are also disorderly! If you listen to the song, you will notice that some parts are calm and melodic, while

---

[185] Francis Schaeffer, *Art and the Bible* (Downers Grove, Illinois: InverVarsity Press, 1973), pp. 7-8.

other parts seem harsh and angry, with a loud guitar and a shouting voice.

> Conversion, software version 7.0
> looking at life through the eyes of a tire hub
> eating seeds as a pastime activity
> the toxicity of our city, of our city
> You, what do you own the world?
> how do you own disorder, disorder
> Now, somewhere between the sacred silence
> Sacred silence and sleep
> somewhere, between the sacred silence and sleep
> disorder, disorder, disorder... [186]

a. How about technical excellence? Since this is not the style of music I usually listen to, it is not easy for me to evaluate it. However, I understand that within this genre, many people consider it well done. b. Is it in harmony with the worldview of the artist? From what I have read on the Internet and seen in a television report, it seems that it expresses the group's worldview. The musicians are angry about war and genocide. Their grandparents witnessed the deaths of family members in the Armenian genocide that occurred between 1915 and 1923 at the hands of the Turks.[187] c. Is the message true? As a Christian, I can't agree with the idea that all things are disorderly, if that is really what they are saying. However, I can agree that there is much corruption in the world. d. Is the form appropriate for the content? Yes, I would have to give

---

[186] System of a Down, "Toxicity", Internet site:
< http://www.elyrics.net/read/s/system-of-a-down-lyrics/toxicity-lyrics.html> (June 1, 2010).
[187] "Screamers," video broadcast on the SCINE channel, September 24, 2007.

them a high score in this area. If they are angry, and if they believe things are disorderly, then they have expressed this very well with the shouting and the loud guitar!

Does this all sound a little too positive? If so, I understand the reaction. I confess that I first felt very negative about this song, and I still don't really enjoy it, frankly. But I wanted to analyze this song exactly for that reason. Even if the song is not my favorite style, I can still admit that the song has redeeming qualities. And even though I don't totally agree with the message of the song, I can still say that I respect the viewpoint of the musicians.

Terry Glaspey

Author Terry Glaspey says, "Experiencing art is like falling in love. It demands vulnerability at the start, and it often takes a lot of work to keep it alive and growing." This means learning to be open to new things and taking our time to appreciate art. He compares this to two kinds of travelers, "pilgrims" and "tourists." A "pilgrim" is not in a hurry, and wants to learn new things about the culture, the food, the people and the customs of the country where he is visiting. A "tourist" is more concerned about keeping an agenda and seeing all the typical things, is often annoyed by inconveniences and becomes exhausted as he rushes through the museums, trying to quickly see all the famous paintings.[188]

I can identify with this. I can be a "tourist" sometimes, but I'm learning to be a "pilgrim". My wife Angelica helps a lot. It took me time to appreciate the *Sagrada Familia* temple in Barcelona, Spain. At first, it just seemed too strange. But after walking around and taking a closer look, I became

---

[188] Terry Glaspey, *Discovering God Through the Arts* (Chicago: Moody Publishers, 2021), pp. 27-34, Kindle Edition.

fascinated by it. I was especially moved by a sculpture of Jesus being tortured. It has taken me time to appreciate musicians like Beethoven. He was never my favorite composer, but one day I was driving alone on a long trip and began to listen to the second movement of his symphony #7. It was absolutely moving, and I listened to it over and over. Only a genius could compose something like that.

Our Attitude toward Art

I believe we should use discernment, but that we should develop a more positive attitude toward art in general. God gives His universal grace, His common grace, to all people, and every human being reflects the image of God.

William D. Romanowski proposes a more open attitude in his analysis of popular culture.[189] He considers that artistic creativity is a gift of God, and quotes John Calvin in his commentary on Genesis.

> The invention of the arts, and other things which serve the common use and convenience of life, is a gift of God by no means to be despised, and a faculty worthy of commendation.[190]

Romanowski finds themes, especially in music and movies, that clearly reflect aspects of Christian doctrine. For example, he says that Bruce Springsteen sings about sin, about temptation, forgiveness, death, and hope, among other things. Without suggesting anything regarding the true spiritual condition of the singer, he says that the presence of

---

[189] William D. Romanowski, *Eyes Wide Open; Looking for God in Popular Culture* (Grand Rapids: Brazos Press/Baker, 2001).
[190] John Calvin, Commentary on Genesis, quoted in Romanowski, *Eyes Wide Open*, p. 55.

these concepts in his songs is due to his catholic upbringing. We should recognize that many movies and television programs show something of the presence of the supernatural, although it is often not a biblical perspective (for example, in the *Harry Potter* series). It is not difficult to think of movies based on the struggle between good and evil, such as *The Gladiator, Braveheart,* and *Schindlers's List.*[191]

Without trying to impose a Christian interpretation where this was not the intention of the producers, the movie *Matrix* clearly illustrates the theme of redemption, including a substitutionary death and a resurrection. At the end of the film, the protagonist gives his life for the others, is resurrected, and destroys the enemy, making use of his new powers. Since Jesus Christ is the greatest hero of all time, it should not surprise us when producers consciously or unconsciously create their heroes to reflect some of His characteristics.

Christian themes appear in secular art because the grace of God reaches all. God has revealed something of His truth to everyone, and even if they try to suppress it, it still manifests itself. According to Romans, chapters one to three, all people know that God exists, they have a sense of right and wrong, and they have a sense of guilt. Man cannot totally erase these concepts from their hearts, because they have been engraved there by their creator. These three aspects alone are sufficient to make hundreds of movies and compose thousands of songs.

Of course, not all art reflects Christian themes. But even when it doesn't, we can still learn something from it. If nothing else, we can see the results of sin, the spiritual emptiness, and the need for God. We need to listen to the

---

[191] Romanowski, *Eyes Wide Open*, pp. 90-120.

insecurity and the despair, in order to learn to show compassion and share the gospel with them.

Kierkegaard explains how pain often produces poetry:

> What is a poet? A poet is an unhappy being, whose heart is torn by secret sufferings but whose lips are so strangely formed that when the sighs and cries escape them, they sound like beautiful music.[192]

We can capture the profound sadness in the paintings of Frida Kahlo from Mexico. She suffered an accident when she was young and lived constantly with pain. But her deeper suffering was sentimental, in her relationship with Diego Rivera, a famous painter of murals. According to her, her marriage was her "second accident," worse than the bus accident. She painted self-portraits with a sad face, with nails in her head, with tears, sometimes with a heart bleeding on her dress.[193]

Art is often an x-ray of the artist himself and of the current social situation. According to Francis Schaeffer, art (especially speaking of painting) is the "second step" in the line of cultural influence, just after philosophy. But he suggests that art touches more people than philosophy.[194]

Our attitude toward secular art becomes more positive when we look for the evidence of the grace of God in it, and when we become more interested in the world around us. We don't have to be so negative, but rather we can evaluate

---

[192] Sören Kierkegaard, *Either/Or*, quoted in *A Kierkegaard Anthology*, ed. Robert Bretall (New York: Random House, 1946), p. 26.

[193] Phyllis Tuchman, "Frida Kahlo," *Smythsonian*, vol. 33, number 8, November, 2002, pp. 51-56.

[194] Francis Schaeffer, *The God Who is There* (Downers Grove, Illinois: Inter Varsity Press, 1998), p. 46.

both the good and the bad. We can learn much from artists, because they are profoundly sensitive people.

We can't be naïve, calling any song that mentions God "Christian" (as some did with the Beatles song "My Sweet Lord," which was actually dedicated to Hare Krishna.) Neither should we expose ourselves to many of the inappropriate things shown to the public today. Paul says in 1 Corinthians 10:23, "All things are lawful, but not all things edify." But we shouldn't lose the opportunity to learn something from art, seeking residues of truth anywhere. We should be like the old gold miners, looking for nuggets of gold in art.

I am afraid that the Evangelical church has lost touch with much of the youth outside. If we stay inside our comfortable groups and ask them to come join us and become like us, most will not be interested. We need to go out to them and listen to them. Jesus left His comfort and His glory to become one of us. He sat at the table with sinners and reached out to touch lepers. We need to learn the cultural language of people outside, in order to understand them. In *The Forgotten Ways*, Alan Hirsch points out that our congregations tend to develop a certain homogeneous identity, which gives easy access only to those who are similar to us. For example, our congregation may be mostly Anglo-Saxon, upper middle class, successful, well-educated families. There is nothing wrong with this, but it might mean that we are not easily approachable by the majority of the population around us. He noticed that his own church in Australia was easily accessible to only around twelve percent of the population, because most of the population was "complex and multicultural."[195]

---

[195] Alan Hirsch, *The Forgotten Ways* (Grand Rapids: Brazos Press, 2006), p. 35.

Jesus and Art

Although the Bible says little about the youth of Jesus, we can imagine that he probably learned to be a carpenter from his earthly father, Joseph. If that is the case, we can also suppose that he was an excellent artist. We can also assume that he enjoyed singing praise songs in the synagogue and reading the poetry of the Old Testament.

Furthermore, remember that the whole creation is His work of art. Speaking of Jesus, Hebrews 1:2 says, "...through whom also he created the world." (See also John 1:2-3.) And when God finished, He was pleased, saying "behold it was very good" (Genesis 1:31). Proverbs indicates how much the Triune God enjoyed this project. Wisdom personified says:

Proverbs 8:27-31

When he established the heavens, I was there; when he drew a circle on the face of the deep, when he made firm the skies above, when he established the fountains of the deep, when he assigned to the sea its limit, so that the waters might not transgress his command, when he marked out the foundations of the earth, then I was beside him, like a master workman, and I was daily his delight, rejoicing *before him always,* rejoicing *in his inhabited world and* delighting *in the children of man.*

Nothing makes me enjoy art more than realizing that God Himself delights in it. Can you imagine Him flinging the stars into space and painting the sky such a pleasant blue? Can you picture Him sculpting the mountains, planting the forests and green pastures, carving the valleys, and pouring out the water to flow through them? Reflect on His profound sense of satisfaction when He designed the perfect details in the jewels, the flowers, and the birds! Above all, think of that deep breath of contentment that He probably gasped when He crowned man himself with glory and majesty (Psalm 8:5). Think of how He continues to stir the clouds in unusual patterns every day and to paint the unique colors of a sunset.

Psalm 104:31

May the glory of the LORD endure forever; may the LORD rejoice in his works.

We can follow His example and delight in our artistic abilities. We can develop hobbies, learn to play the guitar or the piano, to sing, or to paint. The house can be used to display beauty, and the preparation of food and the arrangement of the table can become expressions of creativity. There are many jobs that are worthy of being called artwork, such as jewelry, carpentry, architecture, and design. Every time we enjoy our creativity, we are reflecting the image of God.

Finally, when we open the book of Revelation, we see heaven opened and the promise of future glory. We see an abundance of symbolism and artwork, all centered on Jesus. There are songs of praise, the sound of trumpets, fine clothes, and banquets. There is a new heaven and a new earth, a new Jerusalem with streets of gold, walls of precious stones, the tree of life, and flowing streams. The new creation will be a marvelous work of art, beyond our imagination!

Review Questions
1. Why should a Christian be more interested in art than anybody?

2. What does Rookmaaker want to show in his book, *Modern Art and the Death of a Culture?*

3. What does Rookmaaker say about the reformers' attitude toward art? What caused this attitude?

4. What word does the author use to describe postmodern art?

5. What is Rookmaaker's view of the value of art?

6. What is Dorothy Sayers' opinion about "art" which only entertains?

7. What is the perspective of Francis Schaeffer regarding the value of art?

8. Mention the four guidelines of Schaeffer for evaluating a work of art.

9. What does Terry Glaspey teach us about appreciating art by pointing out the difference between "pilgrims" and "tourists"?

10. What should our attitude be toward art, according to the author?

11. Mention some Christian themes that are often found even in non-Christian music and movies.

12. Why do Christian themes often appear in secular art?

13. Where does Francis Schaeffer put art in his line of cultural influence?

14. In what sense should we be like gold miners when we analyze art?

15. In what different ways was Jesus a great artist?

Questions for reflection

1. What has been your attitude toward art? Has this chapter changed your thinking in any way? How?

2. How would you evaluate the song "Toxicity"? Explain why.

3. What Christian themes, besides the ones mentioned in the chapter, have you found in contemporary music and movies?

4. How would you describe currently popular music?

5. In what ways does Jesus inspire you to develop your artistic abilities?

6. How can you make your life a "work of art"?

Exercise

Talk as a group about a work of art, a movie, or a song. Try to identify what the artist or composer wants to communicate. Use Francis Schaeffer's four standards to evaluate it:

a. Technical excellence. (Is it well done?)

b. Validity. (Was it done in harmony with the artist's approach to life, or just to make money or be accepted?)

c. Intellectual content. (Is the message or approach to life true?)

d. Integrity. (Are the content and form of communication in harmony?)

CONCLUSION

When I walk around our neighborhood, I can easily see which trees are strong, because they stand straight. Others have been shaped by the wind, bending over. My hope is that we can become stronger, able to resist the winds of non-Christian thinking, standing straight. This is not just an intellectual matter; it's spiritual. We are to renew our minds so that we can do God's will (Romans 12:2). Just as we put on our Christian glasses to read the Bible and pray for the Holy Spirit to help us understand His Word, we should keep those same glasses on when we watch the news on TV, read a book, listen to music, or watch a movie.

I don't pretend to have definitive or complete answers for such complex subjects as politics, economics, science and art. And I can't keep up with all the latest writings and trends. I only want to give some guidelines, and share some thoughts, in order to encourage the reader to continue developing a Christian worldview. Nobody has complete intellectual integrity in this life.

However, we can't go to the extreme of some who deny the possibility of knowing the truth. We can identify with Tolstoy when he says,

> If I know the way home and am walking along it drunkenly, is it any less the right way because I am staggering from side to side? [196]

---

[196] Leon Tolstoy, personal letter, quoted by Philip Yancey in *Soul Survivor*, p. 130.

Even though we may stumble, we can be assured that we are on the right road, as long as we keep our eyes on Jesus, "the founder and perfecter of our faith" (Hebrews 12:2).

BIBLIOGRAPHY

Alberta, Tim. *The Kingdom, the Power, and the Glory: American Evangelicals in an Age of Extremism.* HarperCollins. Kindle Edition.

Bahnsen, Greg. *Van Til's Apologetic*. Phillipsburg, New Jersey: P&R, 1998.

Blamires, Harry. *The Christian Mind; How Should a Christian Think?* Ann Arbor, Michigan: Servant Books, 1963.

Blank, Rodolfo. *Teología y misión en América Latina.* [Theology and Mission in Latin America] San Luis, Missouri: Concordia, 1996.

Blomberg, Craig. *Neither Poverty Nor Riches.* Downers Grove: IVP, 1999.

Bonino, José Míguez. *Ama y haz lo que quieras; hacia una ética del hombre nuevo.* Buenos Aires: La Aurora, 1972.

_____ *Christians and Marxists: The Mutual Challenge to Revolution.* Grand Rapids: Eerdmans, 1976.

_____ *Doing Theology in a Revolutionary Situation,* (Fortress Press, Philadelphia, 1975).

_____*La fe en busca de eficacia.* Salamanca: Ediciones Sígueme, 1977.

_____ "New Trends in Theology", Duke Divinity School Review 42 (Fall, 1997):

_____ "The Struggle of the Poor and the Church," *Ecumenical Review* 27 (January, 1975): 38.

Briner, Bob. *Roaring Lambs; A Gentle Plan to Radically Change Your World*. Grand Rapids: Zondervan, 2000.

Calvin, John. *Institutes of the Christian Religion*, ed. John T. McNeill. Philadelphia: Westminster Press, 1967.

Carson, Donald A. *Christ and Culture Revisited*. Grand Rapids, MI: Eerdmans, 2008. Kindle Edition.

Colson, Charles, and Pearcey, Nancy. *How Now Shall We Live?* Wheaton: Tyndale, 1999.

Cooper, Derek. *Christianity and World Religions; An Introduction to the World's Major Faiths*. Phillipsburg, NJ: P&R Publishing, 2013.

d'Epinay, Christian Lalive. *Haven of the Masses; A Study of the Pentecostal Movement in Chile.* London: Lutterworth Press, 1969.

Dockery, David S; Wax, Trevin. *Christian Worldview Handbook*. B&H Publishing Group, 2019. Kindle Edition.

Fischerman, John. *Fearless Faith*. Eugene, Oregon: Harvest House, 2002.

Frame, John. *A History of Western Philosophy and Theology.* Phillipsburg, NJ: Presbyterian and Reformed Publishing, 2015.

_____. *Apologetics; A Justification of Christian Belief.* Phillipsburg, NJ: Presbyterian and Reformed Publishing, 2015.

Fujimura, Makoto. *Art and Faith; A Theology of Making.* New Haven: Yale University Press, 2020.

_____. *Culture Care; Reconnecting with Beauty for Our Common Life.* Downers Grove, IL: IVP Books, 2017.

Giannini, Humberto. *Esbozo para una historia de la filosofía.* [An outline of the history of philosophy] Santiago de Chile, 1981. (First edition published privately.)

Gish, Duane. *Evolution; the Fossils Still Say No!* Master Books, reprinting of 1985 edition.

Glaspy, Terry. *Discovering God Through the Arts; How Can We Grow Closer to God by Appreciating Beauty and Creativity?* Chicago: Moody Publishers, 2021.

Gott, Richard. *Cuba; a New History.* New Haven, CN: Yale University Press, 2004.

Groothuis, Douglas. *Truth Decay; Defending Christianity Against the Challenges of Postmodernism.* Downers Grove: IVP, 2000.

Ham, Ken, Hugh Ross, Deborah B. Haarsma, Stephen C.

Meyer, and J. B. Stump. *Four Views on Creation, Evolution, and Intelligent Design*. Zondervan. Kindle Edition. 2017.

Hansen, Collin, Derek Rishmawy and others. *Our Secular Age: Ten Years of Reading and Applying Charles Taylor*. The Gospel Coalition, 2017.

Hayhoe, Katherine. *Saving Us; A Climate Scientist's Case for Hope and Healing in a Divided World*. New York: One Signal Publishers/Atria Books, 2021.

Hoffecker, W. Andrew, ed. *Building a Christian World View*. Phillipsburg, NJ: Presbyterian and Reformed Publishing, 1986.

Johnson, Paul. *Modern Times: A History of the World From the 1920s to the Year 2000*. Revised edition. Harper Collins, 1992.

MacArthur, John. *Think Biblically; Discovering a Christian Worldview*. Wheaton, Illinois: Crossway, 2003.

Machen, J. Gresham. *Christianity and Culture*. http://homepage.mac.com/shanerosenthal/reformationink/jgmculture.htm

Lewis, C. S. *Miracles*. New York: MacMillan, 1968.

_____. *Surprised by Joy*. Orlando, FL: Harcourt Brace and Company, 1955.

McGovern, Arthur F. *Marxism, an American Perspective*. Maryknoll, New York: Orbis Books, 1980.

Meeter, Henry M. *The Basic Ideas of Calvinism, 6th edition*. Grand Rapids: Baker, 1990.

Middleman, Udo. "Creativity and the Value of Work." http://thirdmill.org/newfiles/udo_middelman/udo_middelman.work.html

Moreland, J.P., and Reynolds, John Mark, eds. *Three Views on Creation and Evolution*. Grand Rapids: Zondervan, 1999.

Morris, Henry. *Science and the Bible*. Chicago: Moody Press, 1986.

Mueller, Walter. *Understanding Today's Youth Culture*. Wheaton, Illinois: Tyndale, 1994.

Myers, Kenneth A. *All God's Children and Blue Suede Shoes; Christians and Popular Culture*. Wheaton, Illinois: Crossway, 1989.

Niebuhr, H. Richard. *Christ and Culture.* New York: HarperCollins, 2001. Originally published in 1951.

North, Gary. Introduction to Christian Economics. Nutley, New Jersey: Craig Press, 1974.

Novak, Michael. *The Spirit of Democratic Capitalism.* New York: Simon and Schuster, 1982.

Oyarbide, Miguel Angel. *Huellas del cristianismo en el arte; la pintura*. Barcelona: CLIE, 2001.

Poythress, Vern. "A Biblical View of Mathematics" in *Foundations of Christian Scholarship; Essays in the Van Til Perspective*. Vallecito, California: Ross House Books, 1976.

_____. *Redeeming Science: a God-Centered Approach.* Wheaton, IL: Crossway Books, 2006.

Poythress, Verne. See the following site for the articles listed below, and others: http://www.frame-poythress.org/
"Redeeming Physics"
"A Biblical View of Mathematics"
"Creation and Mathematics; What Does God Have to do with Numbers?"

Romanowski, William D. *Eyes Wide Open; Looking for God in Popular Culture*. Grand Rapids: Brazos Press, 2001.

Rookmaaker, H.R. *Modern Art and the Death of a Culture.* Wheaton: Crossway, 1994. Originally published in 1970.

_____ *Art Needs no Justification*. Downers Grove, Illinois: InterVarsity Press, 1978.

Ryken, Philip Graham. *Art for God's Sake; A Call to Recover the Arts*. Phillipsburg, NJ: P&R Publishing, 2006.

Sayers, Dorothy. *The Whimsical Christian; 18 essays.* New York: Collier, 1978. Also published as *Christian Letters to a Post- Christian World*. New York: Collier, 1987.

Schaeffer, Francis. *The God Who is There.* Downers Grove: IVP, 1998. Originally published in 1968.

_____. *Art and the Bible.* Downers Grove: IVP, 1973. Republished in 2009.

Sire, James. *The Universe Next Door; A Basic Worldview Catalog.* Downers Grove: IVP, 1997.

Smith, James K. A. *Desiring the Kingdom: Worship, Worldview, and Cultural Formation.* Grand Rapids: Baker, 2009.

Stott, John. *Your Mind Matters: The Place of the Mind in the Christian Life.* IV Books, 2006.

Taylor, Charles. *A Secular Age.* Cambridge, MA: Harvard University Press, 2007.

Trueman, Carl R. *Republocrat; Confessions of a Liberal Conservative.* Phillipsburg, NJ: P&R Publishing, 2010.

Tuchman, Phyllis. "Frida Kahlo", *Smithsonian,* vol. 33, no. 8, Nov., 2002, pp. 51-56.

Unamuno, Miguel de. *Del sentimiento trágico de la vida.* Madrid: Akal, 1983.

Van Til, Cornelius. *The Defense of the Faith.* Phillipsburg, New Jersey: Presbyterian and Reformed, 1979.

_____ *Defense of the Faith; Doctrine of Scripture*.
Phillipsburg, New Jersey, Presbyterian and Reformed,
1967.

Walsh, B.J. y J.R. Middleton. *The Transforming Vision:
Shaping a Christian World View.* Downers Grove, IL: IVP,
1984.

Whitcomb, John C., and Morris, Henry. *The Genesis Flood;
the Biblical Record and its Scientific Implications*.
Phillipsburg, NJ: Presbyterian and Reformed, 1961.

Wolters, Albert M. *Creation Regained; Biblical Basics for a
Reformational Worldview*, second edition. Grand Rapids:
Eerdmans, 2008. Kindle edition.

Yancey, Philip. *Soul Survivor; How My Faith Survived the
Church.* New York: Doubleday, 2001.

INDEX

www.ingramcontent.com/pod-product-compliance
Lightning Source LLC
Chambersburg PA
CBHW060420130626
46555CB00005B/2141